THE WORLD OVER

BY KEITH BUNIN

DRAMATISTS
PLAY SERVICE
INC.

THE WORLD OVER
Copyright © 2003, Keith Bunin

All Rights Reserved

CAUTION: Professionals and amateurs are hereby warned that performance of THE WORLD OVER is subject to payment of a royalty. It is fully protected under the copyright laws of the United States of America, and of all countries covered by the International Copyright Union (including the Dominion of Canada and the rest of the British Commonwealth), and of all countries covered by the Pan-American Copyright Convention, the Universal Copyright Convention, the Berne Convention, and of all countries with which the United States has reciprocal copyright relations. All rights, including professional/amateur stage rights, motion picture, recitation, lecturing, public reading, radio broadcasting, television, video or sound recording, all other forms of mechanical or electronic reproduction, such as CD-ROM, CD-I, DVD, information storage and retrieval systems and photocopying, and the rights of translation into foreign languages, are strictly reserved. Particular emphasis is placed upon the matter of readings, permission for which must be secured from the Author's agent in writing.

The English language stock and amateur stage performance rights in the United States, its territories, possessions and Canada for THE WORLD OVER are controlled exclusively by DRAMATISTS PLAY SERVICE, INC., 440 Park Avenue South, New York, NY 10016. No professional or nonprofessional performance of the Play may be given without obtaining in advance the written permission of DRAMATISTS PLAY SERVICE, INC., and paying the requisite fee.

Inquiries concerning all other rights should be addressed to Creative Artists Agency, 767 Fifth Avenue, 10th Floor, New York, NY 10153. Attn: George Lane.

SPECIAL NOTE
Anyone receiving permission to produce THE WORLD OVER is required to give credit to the Author as sole and exclusive Author of the Play on the title page of all programs distributed in connection with performances of the Play and in all instances in which the title of the Play appears for purposes of advertising, publicizing or otherwise exploiting the Play and/or a production thereof. The name of the Author must appear on a separate line, in which no other name appears, immediately beneath the title and in size of type equal to 50% of the size of the largest, most prominent letter used for the title of the Play. No person, firm or entity may receive credit larger or more prominent than that accorded the Author. The following acknowledgment must appear on the title page in all programs distributed in connection with performances of the Play:

Playwrights Horizons, Inc., New York City,
produced the World Premiere of *The World Over*
Off-Broadway in 2002–2003.

for Peter Parnell

THE WORLD OVER was originally produced by Playwrights Horizons (Tim Sanford, Artistic Director; Leslie Marcus, Managing Director; William Russo, General Manager) in New York City on October 1, 2002. It was directed by Tim Vasen; the set design was by Mark Wendland; the lighting design was by Michael Chybowski; the original music and sound design were by David Van Tieghem; the costume design was by Ilona Somogyi; the fight director was J. Allen Suddeth; and the production stage manager was Jared T. Carey. The cast was as follows:

THE GEOGRAPHER	James Urbaniak
XAVIER, a Cyrillian sailor	Kevin Isola
VINCITORE, a Cyrillian sea captain	Stephen Largay
LORENZACCHIO, a Cyrillian balladeer	James Urbaniak
ADAM, a castaway	Justin Kirk
FERDINAND, King of Gildoray	Matthew Maher
ANSELM, Prince of Gildoray	Stephen Largay
WILHELM, Prince of Gildoray	Kevin Isola
ULRIKE, a lass of Gildoray	Rhea Seehorn
OTTO, physic to Ulrike	Matthew Maher
DARKLY JACK, a pirate	Matthew Maher
ISOBEL, Princess of Peregrine	Mia Barron
CINDRA, a maid attending Isobel	Rhea Seehorn
SATURNIUS, Sultan of Peregrine	Stephen Largay
HIGH PRIEST attending Saturnius	James Urbaniak
KARL, a farmer of Dvolnek	Matthew Maher
RUSELKA, wife to Karl	Rhea Seehorn
TOBIAS, a farmer of Dvolnek	James Urbaniak
THE GRYPHON of Dvolnek	Kevin Isola
NURSE attending Isobel	Rhea Seehorn
OLEANDRA, Empress of Ygrippa	Mia Barron
BARTHOLOMEW, Prince of Magritta	Stephen Largay
EURALIE, Princess of Magritta	Rhea Seehorn
HANIF, a hermit	Matthew Maher
OLD CRONE in a cave	Rhea Seehorn
ROOT, an Amaranthian coachman	Matthew Maher
NICHOLEAUS, a thief	Kevin Isola
AMARANTHA, Queen of Amaranthia	Mia Barron
JOHANNES, Guard to Amarantha	Stephen Largay
LEOCAD, Crown Prince of Leocadia	Matthew Maher
MARGUERITE, a courtesan	Rhea Seehorn
MAMILLIUS, a watch	James Urbaniak
RED-WINGED HAWK	Stephen Largay
MAPMAKER	James Urbaniak
GUARDS, PIRATES, WARRIORS, SAILORS, GENTLEMEN, HERMITS and FISHERMEN	The Company

CHARACTERS

THE GEOGRAPHER
XAVIER, a Cyrillian sailor
VINCITORE, a Cyrillian sea captain
LORENZACCHIO, a Cyrillian balladeer
ADAM, a castaway
FERDINAND, King of Gildoray
ANSELM, Prince of Gildoray
WILHELM, Prince of Gildoray
ULRIKE, a lass of Gildoray
OTTO, physic to Ulrike
DARKLY JACK, a pirate
ISOBEL, Princess of Peregrine
CINDRA, a maid attending Isobel
SATURNIUS, Sultan of Peregrine
HIGH PRIEST attending Saturnius
KARL, a farmer of Dvolnek
RUSELKA, wife to Karl
TOBIAS, a farmer of Dvolnek
THE GRYPHON OF DVOLNEK
NURSE attending Isobel
OLEANDRA, Empress of Ygrippa
BARTHOLOMEW, Prince of Magritta
EURALIE, Princess of Magritta
HANIF, a hermit
OLD CRONE in a cave
ROOT, an Amaranthian coachman
NICHOLEAUS, a thief
AMARANTHA, Queen of Amaranthia
JOHANNES, Guard to Amarantha
LEOCAD, Crown Prince of Leocadia
MARGUERITE, a courtesan
MAMILLIUS, a watch
RED-WINGED HAWK
MAPMAKER

GUARDS, PIRATES, WARRIORS, SAILORS,
GENTLEMEN, HERMITS and FISHERMEN

THE WORLD OVER

ACT ONE

The Geographer, tweedy and affable, in a bit of a rush, stands in front of three large and ancient maps.

THE GEOGRAPHER. The maps in question were exhumed from a cave only this past year. *(He indicates the first map, which depicts a sizeable island divided into one large country labeled* Amaranthia *and one smaller country labeled* Leocadia.*)* This is a representation of the largest land mass in what was then the Alcaden Sea, on the fifteenth of May in the second year of the famous war which divided the island into the two nation–states of Amaranthia and Leocadia. Here in the lower left-hand corner you can see the date and the notarized signature of the mapmaker. *(He indicates the second map, which depicts the same land mass as one unified nation designated as* Adamus.*)* This map is notarized and signed by the same hand. Note that it's dated the sixteenth of May — merely *one day later.* Yet the territory has been transfigured. The nation–states of Amaranthia and Leocadia have been eradicated — and in their place is a new and heretofore utterly unknown country labeled here as *Adamus*. *(He indicates the third map, which is identical in all respects to the first.)* The last map is once again dated merely one day later, on the seventeenth of May. Here you see that the nation–states of Amaranthia and Leocadia have been entirely restored, with their borders and all their topographical features depicted in every respect precisely as they were on the first map. Therefore this conclusion must be drawn: once there was a country called Adamus which existed *only for a single day. (He opens up an old, weathered book and shows us a map that depicts the Straits of Bylorium.)* But how on earth did this come to pass? Here is the question which together we will attempt to answer tonight. And in order to solve the riddle of these

maps, we must first consult an entirely different map, which was drawn up many years earlier and nearly halfway around the world, near an island that as yet had no name. *(Fog. A ship sails into view. Xavier, a green and callow sailor, is atop the mast. Vincitore, the sad-eyed, rueful captain, is at the wheel. Lorenzacchio, an aging, dreamy balladeer, strums a rather baroque guitar-like apparatus.)*
XAVIER. *(In despair.)* Lost.
VINCITORE. Keep watch.
XAVIER. There's no call for a watch when you can't see anything. *(Lorenzacchio's dissonant strumming becomes more obtrusive.)*
VINCITORE. Why don't you go below deck, play a song for my sailors?
LORENZACCHIO. Your sailors won't be calmed by my songs. Half of them believe we're doomed to die out here. The other half are sure we're dead already and this is a ghost ship.
VINCITORE. *(Mordantly.)* Please. If we were dead, at least we'd be at peace. *(A dim light strains through the fog and dances across Xavier's face.)*
XAVIER. A light! I see a — *(Vincitore and Lorenzacchio turn quickly toward the light. Xavier climbs higher atop the mast.)*
VINCITORE. It is — a beacon — !
XAVIER. And there's land!
LORENZACCHIO. *(Stares out across the sea.)* It's an island, I think — *(Vincitore pilots the ship through the choppy waters. The light flickers across Xavier's face.)*
XAVIER. The beacon says bear east — ! *(Vincitore turns the wheel and peers down at the water below.)*
VINCITORE. All these jagged rocks — he's guiding us safely past them —
LORENZACCHIO. Mercy indeed that he saw us — otherwise we'd be ripped to shreds — *(The light changes its direction.)*
XAVIER. Now the beacon says bear west — ! *(Vincitore steers. Lorenzacchio peers down at the water.)*
LORENZACCHIO. And look at the sharks in the sea just waiting to devour us — and there are the hulls of broken ships — ! *(With a thud the ship lands on the coast. They disembark as the fog around them starts to dissipate.)*
VINCITORE. *(Ruefully.)* I'm not used to the earth beneath my

feet anymore — it seems too solid. *(As the last wisps of fog fade away, Adam is revealed. He is dressed all in rags and tatters. He raises his torch in the air and stares at the sailors in wondrous joy.)*
ADAM. Am I saved? *(Xavier draws his sword on Adam.)*
XAVIER. Who's this savage? *(Vincitore motions to Xavier to put up his sword. He moves to Adam.)*
VINCITORE. This is no savage. Here's our navigator.
ADAM. Pray forgive my mean appearance. I must be strange to you. I'm strange to myself.
VINCITORE. Tell us your name.
ADAM. I'm Adam. But till today there wasn't any call for introductions. What a blessing you've landed safely on my shores. Every other ship that attempted the voyage was scuttled on these rocks.
LORENZACCHIO. Yes, between the rocks and the sharks you're quite secure here. Our king would envy your citadel.
ADAM. I'd gladly surrender it to him. It's brought me nothing but grief. The tide is forever washing dead sailors ashore. I bury them in the valley.
VINCITORE. Well, you've steered us safely. Allow us to commend you to your betters.
ADAM. I'm afraid I have no betters.
XAVIER. You can't be the monarch of this island.
ADAM. I'm the monarch, I suppose, and all his subjects too. I'm the only one here.
LORENZACCHIO. How is this possible?
ADAM. Truly I can't tell you. For when I was carried to this place I was an infant. *(He holds out to them the ring he wears upon his finger.)* And the only remnant of my origins is this ring I wear. The old man who piloted our vessel told me it was a gift from my mother. I've been denied all other knowledge of my history.
LORENZACCHIO. But why have you remained so many years in this merciless place?
ADAM. Every day I pray for deliverance from this island. But the ship that carried me here capsized on these rocks. I've endeavored time and again to build another, but the bark on these trees is too weak. I've been a captive here all my life.
VINCITORE. And how have you managed to sustain yourself in this wilderness?

ADAM. I believe in his previous history my guardian was some kind of physic. He was fluent with the roots and bulbs of this island. And he schooled me in the arts of the hunt. By the time he quit this world I was fully educated.
XAVIER. And since then you've lived here all alone?
ADAM. It is I fear a barren life.
LORENZACCHIO. How is it you haven't died of heartbreak?
ADAM. Truly I don't know. All that's sustained me these solitary years is the knowledge that it could only have been the Hand of Heaven that plucked me from the jaws of the sea. And I must've been preserved so I might prove myself someday to be a tremendous hero in the world. I keep myself vigilant for the magnificent hereafter that must be waiting to claim me.
VINCITORE. I'm afraid now it's my regretful duty to declare war on you.
ADAM. I don't understand.
VINCITORE. It seems unfair, I know, especially considering that you've just saved our lives. But we comprise the entire Royal Conquering Navy of the country of Cyrillia. We're conscripted to acquire new colonies for our majesty the king. And our charter mandates us to engage in combat any native population we feel reasonably sure we can subdue. *(Vincitore and Xavier draw their swords. Adam steps back.)*
ADAM. Is there no mercy you can show me? *(Vincitore stops with his sword an inch away from Adam's breast.)*
VINCITORE. I suppose if you surrender willingly, we can make you a prisoner of war.
ADAM. If I become your prisoner, will you carry me away with you?
VINCITORE. Of course.
ADAM. Then I'll happily be conquered. *(Adam kneels before them. Xavier pulls out a thick rope and binds Adam's wrists together.)*
XAVIER. I don't suppose you'll miss this place.
ADAM. *(With a sad laugh.)* The dead I believe hold no fondness for their tombs. *(It's very late at night aboard the ship. Vincitore steers. Xavier is half-asleep at his post atop the mast. Lorenzacchio tunes his instrument. Adam stares down at the water, rapt with fascination.)* It's so strange to look at the sea from on top of the sea.
VINCITORE. I've been at sea so long, it's lost all wonder for me.

ADAM. How many years have you been on this voyage?
XAVIER. *(Sardonically.)* A thousand and two. We're fools of the court, on a fool's errand.
ADAM. I don't understand. *(With a weary sigh, Vincitore takes up his log book. He opens it and shows it to Adam.)*
VINCITORE. Here is a map of Cyrillia. You see it's a tiny country. But our king still wishes an empire for himself. And he lacks the manpower and gold for a proper conquering navy. Instead he's dispatched us to the most obscure and treacherous corners of the globe to place our flag on whatever uncharted land we can find. *(Xavier points down as Adam turns the pages in the log book.)*
XAVIER. So far we've conquered these three islands, those four capes, and that entire archipelago. All of them completely uninhabitable.
LORENZACCHIO. What's worse is, our king was born an invalid. From infancy he's been confined to his bed. He'll never lay eyes on his *own* country, let alone the empire we're building for him.
VINCITORE. But if I value my head I must fill this book with maps and inventories of all his newly acquired lands.
LORENZACCHIO. And I'm required to compose ballads that evoke the more elusive and poetical joys of his holdings.
ADAM. But surely you mustn't keep on with such a bootless mission — you must mutiny, you must abandon ship!
VINCITORE. If it were only so simple. When I was recruited for this voyage my wife was great with our child. Now it's seven years gone and I don't yet know if I have a daughter or a son. I keep my hand to the wheel and my eye on the horizon so one day I might return home and gaze on my family.
LORENZACCHIO. For me it's not so bad. I never had any family who wished to claim me, so I've spent all my days wandering. At least on this voyage I can collect some songs for my trade.
XAVIER. *(Shrugs his shoulders.)* My mother said she couldn't stand the sight of me.
ADAM. But no man's life should be wasted in such purposeless meanderings — we're meant to mark the ground forever with our feet, we're meant to reshape the earth with our hands, so that this world will be a better place for our traveling through it, so that a thousand years from now our names will still be on the lips of

men. We're all of us meant to be heroes. *(Lorenzacchio peers with curiosity at the ring upon Adam's finger.)*
LORENZACCHIO. This jewel you wear — it bears some resemblance to the signet of Gildoray from that old nursery tale.
ADAM. What tale is that?
LORENZACCHIO. It's just a piece of nonsense to put children to bed at night.
ADAM. Pray tell it to me, for I'm starved for stories.
LORENZACCHIO. Well, then: an audience. But I've had no requests for this saga in ages, so you'll forgive me if it's rusty in the telling. *(Clears his throat, takes a deep breath.)* Once upon a time, old King Ferdinand took his twin princes hunting in the wilds on the eastern border of Gildoray. *(As Lorenzacchio speaks, the sea around them is transformed into a dense forest. Ferdinand, deeply self-important, rides into the woods on his horse.)*
FERDINAND. Anselm: easy on the reins. Wilhelm: don't dawdle and lose your way. *(On horseback, the two princes follow him into the woods: Anselm is gentle and noble of bearing. Wilhelm is charmingly incorrigible.)*
LORENZACCHIO. Anselm was delivered from his mother's womb only one minute before Wilhelm. And that was the longest interval this pair had ever spent apart in their lives.
ADAM. I wish I had a twin brother — how marvelous not to emerge friendless into this strange world. *(Ferdinand gathers Anselm and Wilhelm around him.)*
FERDINAND. My boys: I fear this may be my last hunt. For the clock winds down on me. This is the gentle justice of Nature over which even kings hold no sway.
ANSELM. Don't speak of such things, Father.
FERDINAND. Anselm, you're my eldest son, if only by a minute, so when I'm gone you'll be king. Therefore it's imperative that we purchase you a queen. So today we won't just hunt the stag — we'll hunt you a wife as well.
WILHELM. *(To Anselm, with a laugh.)* I've never been so glad to be younger than you, for I want nothing to do with a wife.
FERDINAND. So as we travel through the countryside, should your eye fall on any maiden it desires, convey the girl to me and I'll see you wed at nightfall. *(Ferdinand takes a ring from his pocket*

and hands it to Anselm. Adam stares at the ring, amazed.)
ADAM. This ring is exactly like mine, then?
LORENZACCHIO. Indeed that's how I always imagined the ring to look. All morning the King and his Princes stalked their prey with no achievement. Come noontime they stopped to rest on a jagged rock in the bluffs. *(Ulrike, a sweet and comely peasant lass, appears on the bluffs carrying a bucket.)*
ULRIKE. You men look parched. Would you like some water? *(Anselm and Wilhelm turn to look at Ulrike. They open their mouths to speak but no words come out. They nod eagerly. Ulrike puts the bucket first to Anselm's lips, and then to Wilhelm's.)*
LORENZACCHIO. It seemed to both princes that surely this was the most sumptuous wine that ever crossed their lips. But it was merely well water they drank, so perhaps the alchemy was not in the gift but the giver.
ANSELM. Please tell me your name.
ULRIKE. Ulrike.
WILHELM. Where did this water come from?
ULRIKE. The well on my father's farm. When I was a child I believed the well was enchanted. I'd gaze into its depths for hours. I believed I could see a changeling girl staring back at me. Of course eventually I realized it was my own reflection that fascinated me so, and I chided myself for my vanity. *(Anselm and Wilhelm stare at Ulrike. Then Anselm turns to Ferdinand.)*
ANSELM. Here's the girl I'll marry. *(Anselm takes the ring and places it on the finger of the amazed Ulrike.)*
FERDINAND. You've chosen very wisely. And now we must return to the hunt, for the stag we slay will be your marriage feast. *(Ferdinand rides away. Anselm pulls Ulrike onto his horse with him, and gallops after his father.)*
LORENZACCHIO. Wilhelm was pierced by a thickening ache in his breast. And a malevolent rage festered in his heretofore blameless heart.
WILHELM. *(In fury and anguish.)* My brother will have the whole kingdom! Why does he have to take *her* too?
LORENZACCHIO. At that instant there crept into the glen a baby fawn. The sweet ignorance of the creature seemed to mock Wilhelm even more cruelly. Maliciously he drew his bow and

struck the fawn in the leg. The babe's cries of agony fell strangely pleasant on Wilhelm's ears. And without a second thought he emptied his entire quiver into the beast, and he watched with satisfaction as the life ebbed from the creature's tiny body. *(Wilhelm stands triumphantly over the deer. Ferdinand and Anselm and Ulrike gallop into the clearing. Ferdinand dismounts and tenderly takes the deer in his arms.)*

FERDINAND. *(With a soft cry.)* You've pierced this fawn all through with arrows.

WILHELM. I was — I just —

FERDINAND. *(Whirls on Wilhelm, in fury.)* This babe would've grown into a great stag. It would've borne ten children. When the time was right it would've fed a whole family. Now none of that will ever come to pass. You've made a worthless, spiteful kill. You've ruined everything.

WILHELM. *(Eyes brimming with tears.)* No. No.

FERDINAND. You refuse to live in concert with the natural world. You're not worthy to be my son. I should take your life just as heartlessly as you took this fawn's. *(Ferdinand puts an arrow in his bow and draws it on Wilhelm. Ulrike watches in horror. Anselm dismounts and shields his brother from his father.)*

ANSELM. Father, please — is there no mercy you can show him? *(Ferdinand puts down the bow.)*

FERDINAND. Your brother begs my mercy. So very well: I'll spare your life. But from this day forward and for twenty years hence, you'll live here in the wilds, among the creatures you've used so cruelly.

WILHELM. Father — *(The forest disappears.)*

ADAM. This seems too pitiless a sentence.

LORENZACCHIO. In any event that evening the prince and the peasant girl were married. And the following autumn King Ferdinand passed peacefully out of this life, and Anselm ascended the throne. *(Music. Anselm and Ulrike, dressed in royal finery, dance together.)* The union of King Anselm and Queen Ulrike was joyous but sadly without issue. And on the night of their twentieth anniversary, a servant interrupted their supper to tell them that a tramp stood at the castle gates begging admittance. *(Wilhelm limps into the hall, his hair and tattered clothes covered in twigs and leaves.*

Anselm rises and puts his hand to his mouth.)
ANSELM. Wilhelm?
WILHELM. It's twenty years to the day, isn't it? Am I permitted to beg your forgiveness? *(Anselm goes to Wilhelm and embraces him. Wilhelm stands limp and exhausted, accepting the embrace.)*
ANSELM. You've always had it, whole and entire.
WILHELM. And this must be your queen — she's exactly as I recall — an unparalleled beauty. *(Ulrike comes to Wilhelm and takes him compassionately by the hand.)*
ULRIKE. I'm overjoyed that you're home. *(Wilhelm bows to Ulrike and kisses her hand with utmost tenderness.)*
LORENZACCHIO. And long after the queen retired to bed, the twin princes lingered in the banquet hall. *(Anselm and Wilhelm sit together. Wilhelm holds out a wine cask.)*
WILHELM. I've brought you a present: it's a wine I made myself, from the dirgoberries that grow on the banks of the Falani River. *(Anselm takes a sip of wine.)*
ANSELM. I don't deserve your gifts. It broke my heart when Father banished you. Every spring I sent my men into the wilds to reclaim you, but you wouldn't be found.
WILHELM. It was best I serve my sentence. Indeed the wilds taught me so much our father couldn't.
ANSELM. *(Takes a sip of wine, then:)* Tell me everything you've learned.
WILHELM. *(With very little emotion.)* I've seen the ring-tailed bobcat remorselessly torture a helpless rabbit, devouring it from the legs upward so it remained alive and agonized for as long as possible. I've seen the blue-beaked grouse hatch chicks and then immediately swallow her babies whole. I've learned that Father was mistaken: Nature is cruel, far crueler than I was the day I shot the fawn full of arrows.
ANSELM. *(Coughs slightly.)* I'm afraid Father was mistaken about a great many things.
WILHELM. Even the flowers turn savage when threatened. Consider the dirgoberry: its fruit is pleasing to the eye and sweet to the taste, but even one drop of its wine is fatal poison. *(Anselm opens his mouth to speak but finds he cannot. He puts his hand to his throat.)* It swells and closes your throat: this is why you can't speak.

Soon your body will simply choke itself to death. *(Anselm's face goes red. He wraps his hands around his throat and gasps desperately for air. He manages to eke out one word.)*
ANSELM. Why?
WILHELM. *(Very serenely.)* Because I want your kingdom. And I want your pretty little wife. *(Wilhelm holds Anselm as the life drains from his body.)*
ADAM. I refuse to believe there was ever a man so foul.
LORENZACCHIO. And how many men have you met, exactly? So the next morning Prince Wilhelm declared himself the new king of Gildoray. *(Ulrike, dressed in mourning, is suddenly accosted by Wilhelm.)*
WILHELM. My queen: I convey my deepest sympathies to you in this hour of grief.
ULRIKE. And I to you. It seems unspeakably cruel, that so swiftly you should once again be parted from your brother.
WILHELM. It's a tragic loss for us both. And perhaps we might best bear this loss in concert. May I be so bold as to ask for your hand in marriage?
ULRIKE. *(Struck dumb for a moment, then:)* My husband is barely in the ground.
WILHELM. We're the two he loved most. He'd wish us united.
ULRIKE. I fear I'd profane his memory by taking any other husband. I plan to make a vow of chastity with the sisters of my order.
WILHELM. *(His face hardening.)* I'll grant you a reasonable interval of six months to mourn your king. Then I'll once again ask for your hand. Should you deny me still, I'll wring your neck. *(Wilhelm bows to her and retreats. Ulrike stares after him in horror.)*
LORENZACCHIO. That night the queen became violently ill. She sought the counsel of her loyal physic. *(Otto, a kind, bespectacled physic, appears and examines Ulrike.)*
ULRIKE. I fear I'm dying of grief.
OTTO. You're sick not from grief, but from joy. For the king has left behind an heir.
ULRIKE. *(With a rush of emotion.)* I'll bear my husband's child? This very nearly redeems all my sorrows. But now I'm sick from fear, for should the evil prince learn of this, surely I'll be put to death. He won't have his throne usurped by this infant.

OTTO. I can rid you of the child if that's what you wish.
ULRIKE. *(Shakes her head.)* He's all that's left of my dear Anselm. And he's the rightful king of Gildoray. I'll cloister myself in my chamber. Wilhelm has pledged to forsake my company six months. God willing the baby be delivered by then.
ADAM. This kind old physic — in all respects he's quite like the man who shepherded me to my island.
LORENZACCHIO. And this kind physic prescribed to the queen all the herbs that might speed her delivery, but six months gone and the baby remained in her womb. *(Wilhelm strides into the chamber. Ulrike and Otto turn, startled.)*
WILHELM. I must have your answer: will you marry me?
OTTO. Please, my lord: the queen is not well.
WILHELM. You look quite well to me. Blooming, in fact. Your cheeks are ruddy and your eyes glow golden. Let me touch you. *(Otto steps back as Wilhelm moves to Ulrike. Ardently he caresses her cheek. She stands rigid with fear.)* Haven't you softened to me even slightly? Let me feel your heartbeat. Perhaps it quickens at my approach? *(Wilhelm moves his hand down Ulrike's body. Suddenly he stops.)* Two heartbeats.
ULRIKE. My lord.
WILHELM. *(Nods with understanding.)* It's *his* child. *(Turns to Otto.)* Rip the baby from her body.
ULRIKE. NOOOOOOO! *(Wilhelm goes out. Ulrike wails. Otto lays her on the table.)*
LORENZACCHIO. And the old physic had no choice but to obey his king's command. He carved open the stomach of the poor queen and extracted the barely formed boy from her womb. And he sewed Ulrike up as best he could, and she fell asleep, and he determined it would be merciful if he disposed of the baby's remains before she awoke. *(Otto picks up the tiny child. He stares at it in wonder.)*
OTTO. But what miracle is this? The child breathes. His heart beats so wildly. *(Ulrike rouses herself from sleep. She extends her arms to Otto.)*
ULRIKE. Was that my son?
OTTO. It's your son still — look how much he wants to live. *(Otto places the baby in Ulrike's arms. Ulrike cradles the infant to her chest.)*

ULRIKE. Oh, my child — you won't live long if you remain here.
OTTO. *(With tremendous feeling.)* My Queen: I have a vessel docked at the harbor. I'll conceal the boy and under cover of darkness we'll slip away from this place.
ULRIKE. Heaven bless you for this. *(Ulrike kisses the baby and hands it gently to Otto. She takes the ring from her finger.)* Please, take this ring. When he's old enough, make him a present of it, so he may know his mother loved him beyond measure. *(Otto accepts the ring from Ulrike and withdraws. Adam stares at the identical ring upon his finger.)*
LORENZACCHIO. And the next morning the evil prince once again came to call on the queen. *(Wilhelm enters flanked by guards.)*
WILHELM. I hope the events of this last night have made you forswear your foolishness. Will you have me now?
ULRIKE. Never.
WILHELM. Your husband and your son are already dead. Why do you so fervently wish to join them?
ULRIKE. My son is not dead. He's already long fled from here. And one day he'll return to Gildoray and reclaim his throne. So wring my neck if you wish — I'll die with a smile on my lips because I've set my prince free and clear.
WILHELM. Death would be too merciful for you. *(Turns to his guards.)* Take her to the wilds on the eastern border and abandon her there. *(A guard drags Ulrike from the room. Wilhelm turns to his other man.)* Now: build a giant wall around our borders so no man may come or go from my kingdom without my bidding. And construct a high watchtower so I can stand guard against any invading vessels. And dispatch every ship in our fleet to the four corners of the globe. Find that child and bring him back to me on the point of a sword. *(Wilhelm and the guard vanish. The waves lap against the side of the ship. Adam listens very intently.)*
LORENZACCHIO. A battalion of ships was sent to sea, but the old physic and the child were beyond their recovery. The queen was banished into the wilderness and no one ever heard tell of her again. An enormous tower was indeed constructed, and a watch stands there to this very day, scanning the sea for any signs that the lost prince might be returning to reclaim his kingdom. And —
ADAM. *(In quiet wonder.)* And I am the lost prince of Gildoray.

LORENZACCHIO. *(A bit confused.)* I beg your pardon?
ADAM. *(With mounting excitement.)* You've told me my nativity.
LORENZACCHIO. No, my boy, you don't understand. There *is* no lost prince of Gildoray. Because there is no *Gildoray*. It's just a bedtime tale for children.
ADAM. *(With a new, tremulous joy.)* But here's the proof — this ring was bequeathed to me by my mother the queen — I must rescue her from the dreadful wilds —
LORENZACCHIO. *(Very intensely.)* I didn't say this *was* the ring, I just said it reminded me of what the ring would've *looked* like if it actually *existed* which it *doesn't* because the whole thing is a *romance* —
ADAM. *(Exultantly.)* — and I have to raise an army, I have to take back my country from the false king, I must deliver my people, I must reclaim my throne —
LORENZACCHIO. — and half of that story I just now made up, on the spur of the moment — *(Adam runs to Vincitore and grabs him fervently by the shoulders.)*
ADAM. I order you, Captain, chart a course for Gildoray — it's essential that I get home immediately —
VINCITORE. You're issuing me *orders* now? You're my *prisoner*.
ADAM. *(Euphoric.)* You must divert your course, I beg of you, the fate of an entire nation hangs in the balance, I'm penniless now but once I regain my kingdom I'll give you so much gold —
VINCITORE. And I don't know where Gildoray *is*, I've never even seen the place on a *map* — *(Adam climbs the mast to the crow's nest where Xavier has nodded off.)*
ADAM. *(Jubilantly.)* It's the Hand of Heaven come to make its purpose known to me at last — *(Xavier snaps awake. He peers out on to the sea and lets out a cry.)*
XAVIER. PIRATES! *(All of a sudden the ship is overrun by pirates. Within seconds Xavier and Vincitore and Lorenzacchio and Adam are bound hand and foot. Darkly Jack, leader of the pirates, swarthy and cocksure, strides across the deck, scabbard in hand.)*
DARKLY JACK. Salutations one and all. I hope my men haven't bound you too tightly. Our goal is to subdue but not to scar.
VINCITORE. We're not writhing in agony if that's what you mean.
DARKLY JACK. I'm glad to hear it. My name is Darkly Jack.

Let's clarify the new chain of command: your ship and all your possessions are mine to do with as I please. As are your lives.
XAVIER. Is there no mercy you can show us?
DARKLY JACK. I don't offer mercy. I do however offer employment. The pirate's life is a brutal one. I'm constantly losing men to the sword and the rack and all manner of seafaring diseases. So I'm forever in need of new recruits. Therefore I offer all my captives a choice. Death. Or life as a pirate.
XAVIER. I choose life as a pirate.
DARKLY JACK. *(Considers him very closely.)* A craven little coward, aren't you? Too craven by half. What if *my* ship were attacked? You'd mutiny in a second to save your own skin. There's no loyalty in you. I'm afraid I can't use you. *(Darkly Jack cuts Xavier's throat. He slumps dead to the deck. Adam lets out a cry.)*
ADAM. Monster.
DARKLY JACK. *(Turns angrily on Adam.)* Hold your tongue if you value your hide. *(Sets Lorenzacchio in his sights.)* And what about you?
LORENZACCHIO. *(Trembling in fear.)* I'm no sailor. I'm a storyteller. But perhaps I could sing your men to sleep at night.
DARKLY JACK. *(Muses on this a moment.)* My trade requires me to operate in secrecy. If I bring a balladeer into my employ, he'll compose songs about *me*, and they'll be sung by sailors in every port. It would wreck me. I can't have that. *(Darkly Jack runs his blade across Lorenzacchio's throat. He falls down dead. Adam strains furiously against the ropes that bind him.)*
ADAM. Brute. Fiend. *(Darkly Jack sets the point of his scabbard at the base of Adam's neck.)*
DARKLY JACK. If you don't quiet down I'll kill you right now. I won't give you the luxury of a choice. *(Turns to Vincitore.)* And what about you? You seem an able sailor. You've managed to keep afloat in these dangerous waters. Would you consider joining me? Or are you too much a patriot to abandon your country?
VINCITORE. I have no love for my country. But I can't travel with you.
DARKLY JACK. And why not?
VINCITORE. *(With a simple gravity.)* I've left behind my wife and child in Cyrillia. And when it becomes known that I deserted

my ship for a life of piracy, they'll surely be executed for treason on my behalf. That would murder me far more cruelly than any death you can give me today.
DARKLY JACK. *(Nods briskly.)* Very well then. Death it is. *(Darkly Jack cuts Vincitore's throat. He dies. Adam struggles furiously to loose his ropes.)*
ADAM. Animal. Murderer.
DARKLY JACK. I'm no murderer. I'm a merciful angel. I sweep the earth of the walking worthless. So what will you have: the sea or the grave?
ADAM. *(Holding Darkly Jack in his gaze.)* I will be released from you.
DARKLY JACK. I don't believe I've tendered you that option.
ADAM. Do you see this ring I wear?
DARKLY JACK. In fact it interests me greatly.
ADAM. It was given to me by my mother. It's a royal signet naming me the lost prince of Gildoray.
DARKLY JACK. *(With a dangerous laugh.)* Gildoray? Now you're just having fun with me.
ADAM. I tell you the plain truth.
DARKLY JACK. Gildoray is just a nursery tale to tuck children into bed at night. And *every* boy for a time fancies himself the lost prince. Myself included. But before I was ten I discarded that daydream for more profitable ambitions.
ADAM. Just because Gildoray was a daydream to you, that doesn't mean it's a daydream to the Heavens. For somewhere just beyond the horizon line there's a mass of countrymen aching for deliverance. And you may have fancied yourself the lost prince, but I *am* this boy. The Hand of Heaven has marked me and I will not be detained from my mission.
DARKLY JACK. *(Brought up short.)* You really believe this? Are you mad?
ADAM. *(With a pure clarity.)* This is why you must let me go. For I have my mother to rescue and my father's death to avenge and my people to deliver and my throne to reclaim. You've heard the tale, so you know how dire the consequences will be if I'm kept from my pilgrimage.
DARKLY JACK. *(More and more bewildered.)* But Gildoray doesn't

exist. I've been sailing around the world for twenty years and I've never even seen it on a map.

ADAM. Nevertheless: I see it clear as crystal in my mind's eye. My country is aching for me to save it. You must not deter me. *(Darkly Jack stares at Adam, utterly dumbstruck. He turns to his men.)*

DARKLY JACK. Leave us for a moment. *(The pirates disappear below deck. Darkly Jack and Adam hold each other's unblinking gaze.)* I've sent thousands of souls to their last reward and I've never once doubted that I was performing acts of kindness. But if you are indeed the lost prince of Gildoray — then I'd be the foulest of men to keep you from redeeming the country that abandoned you. *(Darkly Jack unties the ropes binding Adam.)*

ADAM. When I've recovered my throne, you'll be commended for this.

DARKLY JACK. I've got to kill the rest of the sailors and sink this ship. I'll tell my men I cut your throat and threw you overboard. Are you strong enough to swim for shore? *(Darkly Jack picks Adam up in his arms and carries him over to the bow of the ship.)*

ADAM. *(With a laugh.)* I'll swim through a hurricane if it'll bring me an inch closer to Gildoray.

DARKLY JACK. All right, then. Swim! *(He tosses Adam into the sea. The Geographer appears holding the log book open to the map depicting the Straits of Bylorium.)*

THE GEOGRAPHER. This map is taken from a log book drawn up by a Cyrillian sea captain. It inventories all the islands and capes he and his crew acquired as colonies for their king. In the captain's journal, he writes of discovering Adam here — *(Gestures to the map.)* — on the island most recently known as Aspira. This book was discovered in the hull of a sunken Cyrillian ship, two degrees east of the country of Peregrine, which is where we can surmise Adam washed up to shore. *(It's the middle of the night. Adam lies unconscious on the beach. Two cloaked figures bearing lanterns creep stealthily across the sand. They stop when they see Adam. One of the figures steps into the moonlight and pulls back her hood to reveal a tender and kind young woman named Isobel.)*

ISOBEL. Is this boy drowned? *(The other figure removes her hood to reveal Cindra, a pert and cheeky serving girl.)*

CINDRA. I pray you, my princess, keep your distance. *(Adam*

twitches and moans in his sleep. Isobel steps closer to him.)
ISOBEL. No, look — he stirs — he lives. Poor child.
CINDRA. I beseech you, keep to the shadows. Should your father the Sultan catch sight of you here —
ISOBEL. I'll just give the boy some water. I'd not see him delivered from the waves only to die of thirst. *(Isobel removes a canteen from beneath her cloak. She takes Adam in her arms and puts the water to his lips. Adam swallows and wakes.)*
ADAM. Am I in Gildoray?
CINDRA. His fever makes him rave.
ISOBEL. *(To Adam, very gently.)* No, kind sir — you've landed in the country Peregrine.
ADAM. *(Considers her very closely.)* Pray tell me: are you a lady?
ISOBEL. This is the first time anyone has ever cast doubt on the matter.
ADAM. I intend no impertinence. But I've never laid eyes on a lady before. Save my mother, of course, but I was ripped from her arms practically at birth so I have no recollection of her. *(His eyes locked on Isobel's face.)* Are all ladies as fair as you? Or am I spoiled forever in spying you first?
CINDRA. He's a flatterer, this one.
ADAM. I don't mean to flatter — I'm just completely ignorant.
ISOBEL. I suppose I'm as fair as some. But what cruel fortune has denied all ladies the sight of you? And what turn of fate led the sea to lodge you in my arms?
ADAM. This ring I wear — it was bequeathed to me by my mother the queen of Gildoray, so one day I might know my birthright. She's been banished to the darkest wilderness, but I'll cut a swath through the brambles that entrap her, I'll carry her back to her throne.
ISOBEL. *(Deeply touched.)* I have a chain from *my* mother. She died the day I was born. Do you see? Inside this chain is another, and another inside that — gifts for my children and their children and all the children beyond. *(Adam takes the chain from Isobel.)* But I've never heard tell of Gildoray. I've never even seen it on a map.
ADAM. I've not laid eyes on it myself. But it's a beauteous country, fair and verdant, bordered on the east by an untameable wilderness and on the west by an emerald sea. From the highest

peak of the Veritian Mountains you can see as far as the Maltavi Plains. And if you wade downstream in the Falani River, you can reach up and pick an apple from the orchard on the edge of the Ingreven Forest.

ISOBEL. How do you see the place so well if you've never laid eyes on it?

ADAM. I see what I'll make of it. Might I beg a favor of you? Can you convey me to any kind nobleman who'd be good enough to lend me a ship from his fleet?

ISOBEL. My poor castaway — how I wish you'd washed up on less perilous shores. If you have any strength left, dive back into the surf and don't come up for air until you're far away from here.

ADAM. What dangers are in this place?

ISOBEL. Our land is ruled by a tyrannical sultan who makes slaves of all his subjects. And travelers like you he burns at the stake just to feed his foul whims.

ADAM. Is there no member of the royal family who might intercede for me?

ISOBEL. *(After a moment's hesitation.)* The Sultan has a daughter called Isobel. But from dawn till dusk he keeps her imprisoned in a cell.

ADAM. Why would he do such a monstrous thing?

ISOBEL. Some claim he bears no love for her. Others say he adores her too greatly to let her be defiled by the world. For myself I don't venture a guess. There's some cruelty that's beyond reason.

ADAM. And has she no respite from this torture?

ISOBEL. Only this: after midnight, when the Sultan is asleep, she slips out her window. She garbs herself in peasant's weeds and walks with her loyal chambermaid along the beach. For a brief hour she can wander the countryside unfettered and enthralled. *(Adam stares at Isobel. His eyes widen in comprehension.)*

ADAM. I'd rescue this princess, if indeed there's any way to rescue her.

CINDRA. There *is* a way.

ISOBEL. Cindra: *enough.*

ADAM. No, tell me, I beg you.

CINDRA. The Sultan has issued a challenge: any young nobleman who wishes the hand of the princess can win her should he

pass three trials.
ISOBEL. But the trials are impossible to pass: there's a riddle no man can solve, and a task no man can perform, and a vow no man can take. And every suitor who fails is beheaded. Fifty-one men have made the pilgrimage. And fifty-one men have lost their heads. The Sultan takes relish in their torture — it's a diabolical game.
ADAM. But if there's any chance to win this poor girl's liberty — then I must make the attempt.
ISOBEL. She's not worth such a hopeless sacrifice.
ADAM. I believe she'd be worth the lives of a million men, if only she were precisely as beautiful as you are.
ISOBEL. Her beauty wanes by the hour — the horror of her confinement robs her of her bloom. But this is providence: soon she'll be so withered that no more men will die for her. And not long after that, she herself will perish, and that will be the greatest mercy of all.
ADAM. *(Considers her very closely.)* Once, when my father was hunting, a girl brought him water. And that very day he made her his queen. Until this moment I didn't believe a man could choose a wife so swiftly. But now I understand how mistaken I was, for I wish to see all the rest of my days reflected back at me in your eyes. *(Turns to her gently.)* It's decided, then. At dawn I'll ask the Sultan for your hand.
ISOBEL. But why? I'm nothing to you.
ADAM. You're my queen. You just don't know it yet. *(At dawn Adam marches up the red carpet to the throne that bears Saturnius, corpulent, maliciously gleeful. Isobel stands nervously behind her father.)*
SATURNIUS. You've come to petition this court for my daughter?
ADAM. *(Bowing before them.)* It's my honor.
SATURNIUS. You appear before me in rags. Is this some kind of insolence?
ADAM. I beg the Sultan's pardon, but for the moment I'm at loose ends.
SATURNIUS. I trust you are indeed a nobleman. For I'd sooner throw my daughter to the wolves than give her to a commoner.
ADAM. I'm the lost prince of Gildoray.
SATURNIUS. We don't often entertain envoys from imaginary nations.

ISOBEL. You see, Father, he's completely insane. Turn him away.
ADAM. If I am out of my wits — I'm sure it would entertain Your Majesty greatly to watch a madman attempt these tests.
SATURNIUS. *(Very pleased.)* It would certainly pass the time. Now this is all very simple. You must solve a riddle. You must perform a task. And you must take a vow. And should you fail to complete any of these trials your head will be separated from your body. *(With a flourish Saturnius indicates his executioner, who sharpens his blade. Adam shudders.)*
ADAM. And when I succeed I'll have Isobel.
SATURNIUS. Oh, yes, absolutely. So here's the riddle: five exit and nine enter, two pour and one drinks, and the one may make one but one day will be multitudes. And this one is in your hands but may slip through your fingers. What is the one?
ISOBEL. I pray you, think on it a while, it isn't so simple.
ADAM. *(Muses a moment.)* Five exit and nine enter. The five days of a woman's bleeding exit. And then enter nine months where she carries a child.
ISOBEL. *(Under her breath.)* He begins with great promise.
ADAM. Then the two that pour are the mother's breasts, and the one who drinks is the baby —
SATURNIUS. *(With gleeful anticipation.)* A baby, then? Is that your answer — a baby?
ADAM. *(Shakes his head.)* Not just any baby — for the one may make one and one day become multitudes — and what does that mean? Only a woman can make another, for only a woman can bear a child. So it's a woman.
SATURNIUS. *(With great displeasure.)* Very good.
ADAM. And only a princess will one day become multitudes, because when she's crowned queen she'll be a whole kingdom. And if the princess is in my hands but may slip through my fingers — well, then the princess must be Isobel, for she's in my hands now but she'll slip through my fingers should I fail these trials. I've passed the test then: Isobel is the answer.
ISOBEL. *(With a quiet joy.)* Indeed I am.
ADAM. That trial was far too simple — for in my present state of mind, Isobel is the answer to everything.
SATURNIUS. Then you'll find the second trial even simpler — for

all I ask you to do is cross this room and take Isobel in your arms.
ADAM. Just that?
SATURNIUS. Just that. Of course you know how much I adore my daughter, so I'd only give her to a man who'd risk life and limb for her.
ADAM. Naturally.
SATURNIUS. So you won't begrudge me if I place a few obstacles in your path. *(Turns to his guards.)* Bind her hands. *(A net falls from the ceiling. The guards grab her and bind her hands into the net.)* Turn the winch. *(Isobel is hoisted off the ground.)* Open the pit. *(A pit is opened, revealing a fiery chasm precisely below the spot where Isobel hangs.)* Now call forth the warriors. *(Three warriors place themselves around the pit.)*
ADAM. What is all this?
SATURNIUS. As I said, all you have to do is cross the room and take Isobel in your arms. But beware: the path to her is guarded by my fiercest warriors. And they won't hesitate to break your neck to keep you from her. Further I pray don't tarry too long in your task. For your love hangs suspended over a pit of burning coals. And when I blow this whistle, four hungry rats will be released. Within a minute they'll gnaw through the net and she'll plunge to her death in the fire below.
ADAM. This must be a trick. For if any man before me failed at this trial, Isobel would be in her grave already.
ISOBEL. *(Dangling helplessly by her arms.)* No man before you even solved the riddle.
ADAM. And I can't believe you'd wager so cruelly with her life.
SATURNIUS. Perhaps I'd rather surrender her to death than to you.
ADAM. *(Whispers nervously to himself.)* The Hand of Heaven has marked me — I won't be vanquished. *(Saturnius blows the whistle. Adam tries to approach Isobel, but the first warrior is upon him. With a deft maneuver Adam flips the warrior on his back. The warrior writhes in agony.)* Is the fair over? Why, I've not sold half my wares.
SATURNIUS. The battle is far from won — she's not yet in your grasp. *(The second warrior attacks Adam and quickly gets him in a headlock. Adam struggles and strains. He manages to kick the warrior in the groin. The warrior is disoriented for just long enough that Adam can land a punch on his jaw. The warrior falls to the ground,*

wailing in pain.)
ADAM. On my island I wrestled bears and lions — this sport is too easy.
SATURNIUS. You fight bravely, but take care, now she hangs only by a thread. *(The third warrior comes at Adam like a ton of bricks and easily pins him. Adam struggles and strains but cannot get free. Slowly the warrior begins to push Adam toward the open pit. Adam stares in helpless horror. At the edge of the pit, the warrior reaches down to pick up Adam and hurl him into the chasm. With one last ounce of strength Adam grabs the warrior and flips him over. The warrior loses his balance and falls, wailing as he descends into the abyss.)* But all your efforts come to nothing — the rope is frayed through. *(Adam looks up just as Isobel falls. Adam extends his arms out over the pit and catches her. Exhausted and triumphant he stands holding Isobel in his arms. The two surviving warriors hobble away. The guards quickly close up the pit. Saturnius considers Adam.)* You're far stronger than I imagined.
ADAM. I'm not half so strong. It's the prize that inspired me. *(Adam gently puts Isobel down. They stand together facing Saturnius.)*
SATURNIUS. Nevertheless, I commend you on your fortitude. And I'll grant you a special dispensation — I invite you to forfeit the last trial, and to leave here forever with your life.
ADAM. Why should I leave now when I'm so close to winning Isobel?
ISOBEL. Accept his offer, please — for your own sake.
ADAM. I'm not afraid of anything.
SATURNIUS. *(Nods, then, to his guards.)* Call forth the high priest.
ADAM. *(Turns to Isobel.)* Is this the vow no man can take?
ISOBEL. It's our wedding vow. *(Adam stares dumbfounded at Isobel as the high priest, a wizened old man, appears in the room bearing two silver chalices. He prays for a moment and then extends his arms to Adam and Isobel.)*
HIGH PRIEST. The gods demand a drop of blood from the nape of this boy's neck. *(The high priest withdraws a large dagger from beneath his robe. Adam looks to Isobel nervously.)*
ISOBEL. It's our custom here. *(Adam moves to the high priest. He pricks Adam's neck with the dagger. Adam lets out a small yelp of pain.*

The high priest lets a drop of blood fall into the chalice. He swirls the blood around and stares at it.)
HIGH PRIEST. His blood is clean. Now the gods demand the same from the girl. *(After a moment's hesitation Isobel moves to the high priest, who pricks Isobel's neck and lets the blood fall into the other chalice. He swirls the blood around and stares down at it.)* The bride's blood is tainted and besmirched.
ADAM. I don't understand.
HIGH PRIEST. She's defiled herself with another.
ADAM. This is some cruel trick. *(Saturnius goes to Isobel and kisses her on the mouth.)*
SATURNIUS. Now you see my great shame: I've brought a succubus into this world, who'd coldly lure a decent man to his degradation. Surely you can't cleave yourself to this horror. *(Adam stares at Isobel trapped in her father's embrace. He nods in sad comprehension.)*
ADAM. Late at night on my island, I'd lie awake and listen to the howling of the beasts. Their cries were horrible beyond my comprehension. I came to believe that after midnight goblins inhabited their bodies, driving them mad from within. I know there are terrible things in the dark. I believe one of these ghouls possessed my Isobel. I know she's blameless in all this. *(Isobel looks up from the ground. Adam turns to the high priest.)* I can't be forbidden to marry her, can I?
HIGH PRIEST. Your union won't be blessed.
ADAM. I require no blessings save the ones we bestow on each other. *(Adam reaches out his hand toward Isobel. She hesitates a moment. Then she moves toward him. Saturnius lets out a cry. He grabs Isobel. He unsheathes his sword and places it to her neck.)*
SATURNIUS. I'll set this knife to her neck before I'll let you take her — !
ISOBEL. *(With a fierce wail of anger.)* Father! Use your eyes! Can't you see that death would be nothing to me? And can't you see that no matter what you do, this boy has already claimed me?
SATURNIUS. *(Taken aback a moment.)* Isobel — my own —
ISOBEL. I'm yours no longer. I belong to the lost prince of Gildoray.
SATURNIUS. *(Sputtering with rage.)* You can't possibly choose this *madman* over me — you'll be without a *home* — the land he

comes from doesn't even *exist.*
ISOBEL. *(With a great fervor.)* You're wrong about that. It's a beauteous country, fair and verdant, bordered on the east by an untameable wilderness and on the west by an emerald sea. From the highest peak of the Veritian Mountains you can see as far as the Maltavi Plains. And if you wade downstream in the Falani River, you can reach up and pick an apple from the orchard on the edge of the Ingreven Forest.
SATURNIUS. Such a place is not to be found on any map.
ISOBEL. *(With a simple clarity.)* I've found it already. I'm living there now. *(Suddenly Saturnius bursts into tears. He falls to the floor, bawling like a baby.)*
SATURNIUS. If I lose you I'll die of grief.
ISOBEL. Then as we speak you must be perishing.
SATURNIUS. *(Defeated, raises his head.)* My sweet Isobel: I've tried to love you as best as I know how. I beg you not to banish me forever from your thoughts.
ISOBEL. *(With a sad laugh.)* Oh, Father — you'll be in my dreams every night.
SATURNIUS. *(Clasps Adam's hands in his own.)* And my boy: I place my daughter in your hands. I pray only that you give her the care she so richly deserves.
ADAM. She'll be safe with me. *(Adam takes Isobel in his arms and kisses her. She throws her arms around him. He picks her up and carries her out of the castle. The Geographer unfurls a scroll which bears a map depicting the country of Peregrine.)*
THE GEOGRAPHER. Here is a map of Peregrine and its bordering nations, hand-inked on a scroll bearing the royal seal of the Sultan. Roughly translated from the original, this legend reads: "The Sultan of Peregrine invites all eligible noblemen to travel to his kingdom and compete in feats of strength and skill — the victor shall claim his daughter Isobel, widely acknowledged to be the most beautiful princess in all the world." Judging from this map, most likely Adam and Isobel would have journeyed west out of the palace. Therefore within several months they would have crossed the border into what was then the marshland country of Dvolnek. *(In the marshy grasses of Dvolnek, a peasant woman named Ruselka lies wailing and screaming on the ground. Her husband Karl, gentle*

and meek, tends to her.)
RUSELKA. AAAAAAAAH! AAAAAAAAAH! *(Adam and Isobel ride through the marsh. Adam dismounts his horse.)*
ADAM. Is this lady sick?
KARL. *(Shakes his head.)* My wife is having a baby. *(Isobel dismounts and kneels on the ground next to Ruselka.)*
ISOBEL. Is there anything we can do to help?
KARL. Please hold her. *(Isobel holds Ruselka and strokes her hair as she cries in pain. Adam kneels down next to Karl and stares at the child emerging from Ruselka's body.)*
ADAM. *(In wonder.)* What's this? Look at this beautiful child —
KARL. *(As soothingly as possible.)* It's all right, Ruselka, soon it'll all be over — *(Tobias, a slightly older peasant, comes running through the grass carrying a knife.)*
TOBIAS. I'll cut the cord for you and then I'll get the baby as far away from her as possible —
ISOBEL. You're almost there — just one more push — *(Ruselka pushes and the baby fully emerges from her body. Tobias cuts the cord. Adam takes hold of the baby and holds it up triumphantly.)*
ADAM. Look at your son —! *(Adam holds out the baby to Ruselka. She covers her face with her hands.)*
RUSELKA. Get him away from me! Don't make me look at him! Why do you delight to torture me?
KARL. *(Whirls angrily on Adam.)* You fool — take the baby away — hasn't my wife suffered enough? *(Karl holds Ruselka in his arms and comforts her. Tobias takes the baby from Adam.)*
ISOBEL. But what kind of mother doesn't even want to look upon her child?
TOBIAS. You're strangers here. You don't understand. High atop that mountain resides a monstrous gryphon.
ADAM. But gryphons exist only in stories.
KARL. That's what I thought too, until one came to live in our country.
RUSELKA. *(Through her tears.)* He makes us surrender our babies for him to feast upon.
ISOBEL. *(Stares up at the mountaintop.)* Oh, no.
TOBIAS. *(Doffs his cap in sorrow.)* My wife was delivered of a daughter last April. She made the mistake of gazing on it for just a

second before it was snatched away for the gryphon to devour. Since that day she hasn't swallowed a crumb of food and she hasn't uttered a single word. She's almost nothing. In a way I envy her.
ADAM. But why don't you fly this place?
KARL. If any man even dares to approach the border, the gryphon swoops down and crushes him with his paw.
RUSELKA. Pray he hasn't yet spied you or else you're trapped here too.
ADAM. Then someone must climb to the top of the mountain and cut off the gryphon's head.
TOBIAS. A few have ventured to try. None have returned. For this beast bears the gift of prophecy — he foresees every step his opponent will take. *(Adam considers Karl and Ruselka and then the baby Tobias holds. Then he nods with firm resolution.)*
ADAM. Nevertheless I must make the attempt.
TOBIAS. But this is madness. *(Adam takes the baby from Tobias and carries it tenderly over to Karl and Ruselka. They stare at him.)*
ADAM. My own murder was decreed before I was born. And I was only preserved by a stranger's courage. I've held this child in my arms. He wants so desperately to live. I'm happy to wager my own life so I might grant him that gift. *(Adam puts the baby in Ruselka's arms. The peasants stare, amazed. Ruselka turns to Isobel.)*
RUSELKA. I beg you — entreat your husband not to wage such a hopeless war.
ISOBEL. If he didn't wage hopeless wars I wouldn't be saved myself. *(Adam kisses Isobel tenderly on the mouth.)*
ADAM. The Hand of Heaven is guiding me to my kingdom. No monster can deter me.
TOBIAS. *(Handing him his knife.)* You'll need a weapon. *(As he reaches the mountaintop Adam comes upon The Gryphon of Dvolnek. The gryphon is a fearsome creature. But when he speaks his tones are world-weary and deeply ironic. He sniffs the air, expelling an angry puff of smoke at Adam.)*
GRYPHON. Where's the baby?
ADAM. Safe and sound down in the valley. *(The gryphon uncoils his tail and examines Adam with grim suspicion.)*
GRYPHON. You're a stranger to me.
ADAM. My wife and I are riding homeward through this country.

GRYPHON. This country *is* your home now. You belong to me.
ADAM. I thought you were only in stories. *(The gryphon extends his neck in puffy satisfaction.)*
GRYPHON. It was my strategy to make your race believe that I am the stuff of legend. This way I can slip obscured through the world, but should I choose to make myself known, my reputation precedes me. You know just enough about me to be properly terrified. *(Considers Adam very closely.)* You've come here to kill me.
ADAM. That's right.
GRYPHON. I'm so weary of you warriors. I don't wish you murdered. I'd much rather you were down in the valley, making babies for me to eat. I won't assail you. But if you come near me with that pathetic little knife I'll strike you dead. Do I make myself clear? *(Adam nods. He circles the mountaintop, searching for a way to get close enough to the gryphon.)*
ADAM. When did you develop such a taste for babies?
GRYPHON. They go down very easily. One or two bites at most. Plus if you wish to enslave a nation, the best course is to devour their young. Take away a man's future, strip him of all his hopes for a legacy, and he becomes quite … docile.
ADAM. I understand that you can divine the future.
GRYPHON. An exaggeration. It's just that when you've lived as long as I have, the future loses its capacity to surprise.
ADAM. Does *my* future present itself to you so easily?
GRYPHON. *(Frowns, considering.)* Let me look into your eyes. *(Adam steps closer to the beast, his hand hovering near his sword. The gryphon peers into Adam's eyes.)* You're a foundling child, am I right? A piece of refuse scattered to the wind. But to the depths of your soul you fancy yourself a hero — perhaps even a king. Beware: these delusions of grandeur you hold so dear may inspire you to feats of stupid bravery and daring, but in the end they'll be your defeat and your despair. *(Adam stares at the gryphon. Then he puffs out his chest and speaks defiantly.)*
ADAM. I'm the lost prince of Gildoray.
GRYPHON. *That* old story! But how ridiculous! Let me put it this way: I'm supposed to be mythical myself, and even *I* don't believe in it.
ADAM. *(With tremendous intensity.)* I promise you: if you gaze

deep into my eyes, you'll see my benevolent hereafter staring back at you. You'll see me as an old king, standing atop a verdant hill, with my children gathered around me, tenderly surveying the country that is my own. *(Adam steps right up to the face of the gryphon. The gryphon frowns and stares deeply into Adam's eyes. They hold each other's gaze for a tense moment.)* So: what do you see? *(The gryphon stares gravely at Adam. Then he bursts into hysterical and uncontrollable laughter.)*

GRYPHON. You don't wish to know. You do not wish to know. *(The gryphon doubles over, howling with rabid, maniacal laughter. Enraged, Adam unsheathes his blade. The gryphon is laughing too madly to even notice. With tremendous force Adam plunges the blade into the gryphon's eye. The gryphon cries out in pain. Smoke belches from his nostrils as he writhes in agony. Slowly the life drains out of him. Adam raises his sword and slices off the head of the gryphon. Adam takes the severed head of the beast in his hands and marches down the hill to where Isobel and Tobias and Ruselka and Karl and the other farmers of Dvolnek are gathered.)*

ADAM. I've brought you a piece of your monster!

KARL. Bring us the rest of him! We'll carve him up and serve him for supper! *(Cheers from the farmers. Isobel beams at Adam. Tobias approaches him, doffs his cap, and kneels.)*

TOBIAS. You've delivered us — we're forever your servants. *(Adam takes Tobias by the hand and raises him up from the ground.)*

ADAM. You mustn't make an idol of me.

RUSELKA. We'll do more — we'll make you our king! *(Tremendous and overwhelming cheers from the farmers. Adam raises his hands for quiet.)*

ADAM. It's such a tremendous honor that you'd bestow on me. But I can't accept it. If you'd be so generous as to provide me with a ship from your fleet so I might continue my pilgrimage — that would be more than recompense enough. *(Adam is embraced in turn by all the grateful farmers. Isobel stands apart. Adam goes to her and takes her gently by the hand. She turns.)*

ISOBEL. Adam: will you walk with me a ways?

ADAM. Of course. *(Isobel leads Adam up a small hill toward a beechnut tree.)*

ISOBEL. This land is passing fair, wouldn't you say?

ADAM. Far more than passing.
ISOBEL. And the people here are gentle, don't you agree?
ADAM. They're the soul of kindness.
ISOBEL. I owe you my life. In all ways I gladly bind myself to your will. But may I be permitted to beg one favor of you?
ADAM. Anything.
ISOBEL. Let's end our travels here.
ADAM. But my love, we're so close to home — !
ISOBEL. I fear the road ahead is long and treacherous. And I ache of this vagabond life.
ADAM. Just let me take you in my arms — I'll carry you all the way.
ISOBEL. But no one seems to know if such a country as Gildoray even *exists* — let alone if you're truly its prince. What if we scour the four corners of the globe and the place won't be found?
ADAM. Isobel: do you doubt me too?
ISOBEL. Perhaps Gildoray is just another name for Paradise. And if it is, you've already built Gildoray in your mind's eye, and I'll gladly live there with you forever. You're a wondrous man: I won't let you squander your days in pursuit of a shadow.
ADAM. It's no shadow — it's my country, desperate for us to deliver it.
ISOBEL. I entreat you, think a moment: you wished for a kingdom of your own. And today one has been offered to you. Surely this is sufficient.
ADAM. *(Thinks a moment, then.)* But this can never be my home.
ISOBEL. *(Quietly heartbroken.)* Are you quite certain of that?
ADAM. I must carry my mother back to her throne. I must break the chains of my countrymen. If I remain here, I abandon them forever. I beg of you, don't wish me that.
ISOBEL. But it's not only for my sake that we must end our travels. For I believe I'm growing great with your child.
ADAM. *(With an amazed joy.)* Our child?
ISOBEL. Yes.
ADAM. *(Throws his arms around Isobel.)* Then we must not tarry here even for a second! We must hoist our sails at once! Our son must be born in his home country. I have no wish to bring any more wanderers into the world.
ISOBEL. But I fear any further journey might risk our baby's life.

ADAM. *(Places his hand on her belly.)* The Hand of Heaven is upon all of us now. I'll protect you.

ISOBEL. *(A long moment, then:)* Is this truly what you wish?

ADAM. *(Kisses her on the mouth.)* We're bringing a new prince home to Gildoray. *(Aboard ship, Adam peers out at the horizon as his sailors bustle around him. A very pregnant Isobel walks the deck guided by her nurse. The sky above is grey and ominous.)*

FIRST SAILOR. Sir, I'm begging you — we must turn back at once.

ISOBEL. *(To her nurse.)* I ache all over.

NURSE. If you keep walking it'll ease your pain. *(Another sailor calls down to Adam from his perch at the crow's nest.)*

SECOND SAILOR. We're entering uncharted waters, sir. *(Adam puts down his glass and runs over to a third sailor who stands at a table surrounded by charts and maps.)*

THIRD SAILOR. It's true — where we are now — it isn't marked on any map.

ADAM. Then we've nearly reached our destination. For Gildoray has to be found somewhere in this ocean. *(Suddenly Isobel doubles over and clutches her belly in pain.)*

ISOBEL. AAAAAAAAAH!

NURSE. It's time — it's time — ! *(The nurse lays Isobel on the deck of the ship. Adam stares at her in wonder, and then turns to look at the horizon line.)*

ADAM. What's that? That shoreline there, in the east?

THIRD SAILOR. I don't know, sir — I don't even know where we are *now* — *(Adam cries out to the fourth sailor, who mans the wheel.)*

ADAM. It's Gildoray, then — it must be Gildoray — full speed ahead!

FOURTH SAILOR. Yes, sir! Right away, sir!

ADAM. My son must be born in his home country!

ISOBEL. AAAAAAAAAH! *(A flash of lightning and a clap of thunder. Everything goes black. When our view is restored it's a few hours later — night has fallen around them. The wind is squally and blustery. The sea is choppy and tempestuous. The sailors are in a panic. Adam stands firmly at the ship's bow.)* AAAAAAAAAH!

NURSE. Just one more push, miss, and he'll be yours —

SECOND SAILOR. A storm is rising in the east — a hurricane, sir!

ADAM. *(Turns to the fourth sailor.)* We can harness the wind —

if we steer into it then surely it'll carry us straight to Gildoray!
ISOBEL. AAAAAAAAH! *(The nurse holds up a tiny infant in her arms.)*
NURSE. A boy! You have a son, miss! You have a son! *(The third sailor calls down from the crow's nest in panic.)*
THIRD SAILOR. The tempest, sir — it's bearing down directly upon us — !
ADAM. *(Turns to the fourth sailor.)* You can't turn back now! We have to keep going!
ISOBEL. *(Cries out with new pain.)* AAAAAAAAH! *(The nurse looks down at Isobel in amazement.)*
NURSE. My lady, you have another child inside you — twice blessed —
FOURTH SAILOR. Sir, we must turn back — the hurricane — it'll swallow us up —
ADAM. I refuse to turn back — not when I'm so close to home — give me the wheel! *(Adam takes the wheel from the fourth sailor as Isobel wails in pain.)*
ISOBEL. AAAAAAAAH! *(A flash of lightning. A crash of thunder. Everything goes dark. When our view is restored everything is chaos. Waves cascade over the sides of the deck. The sailors cry out in panic. Isobel lies weeping as the nurse tries to hold her down. Through it all Adam stands at the wheel.)* AAAAAAAAH!
FIRST SAILOR. It's all over, sir — there's nothing more you can do — if you don't abandon this ship you'll surely die —
NURSE. *(To Isobel.)* Whatever strength you have, miss —
ADAM. I'll keep you safe — don't worry — I'll keep everyone safe — ! *(Isobel gives one last push. A crack of thunder very close by. The ship rises into the air, tossing and turning on the sea.)*
ISOBEL. AAAAAAAAH!
NURSE. You have a daughter, miss — two beautiful children — *(The nurse holds out the two babies to Isobel as a shower of hail descends from the sky.)*
SECOND SAILOR. Abandon ship! Abandon ship! *(Some of the sailors run to the edge of the deck and dive into the sea. Isobel opens the locket in the chain around her neck. She places the two chains inside it around the necks of her babies.)*
ISOBEL. Oh, my babies, wear these jewels about your necks —

so if we're separated you may know your mother loved you beyond measure — !

ADAM. I am the lost prince of Gildoray and I am coming home at last! *(A bolt of lightning strikes the ship, cracking the hull into bits. What few sailors that remain are hurled mercilessly overboard. The pieces of the ship are tossed to and fro. A giant wave washes over Isobel. Adam turns in horror as the babies are ripped from her arms and swept away by the current. Another bolt of lightning strikes the shard of deck where Isobel stands. Adam watches helplessly as Isobel is thrown from the ship and cast into the depths of the sea. The thundersquall blasts through the air. Bolts of lightning parachute from the heavens. Adam lets out a howl of fathomless agony but even his cries cannot be heard above the wind and the rain.)*

ACT TWO

The Geographer pulls down a map depicting the Octavian Ocean and the surrounding continents.

THE GEOGRAPHER. To resume. The navigational chart you see before you is taken from a sailor's almanac that is on generous loan to us from the Nautical Society. It depicts the perceived trajectory of the hurricane Clementia on its unprecedented path of destruction across the Octavian Ocean. Under the assumption that this is the storm which scuttled Adam's ship, we can state with reasonable assurance that he was most likely deposited here — *(Points to the map.)* — on the shores of the jungle nation of Ygrippa. *(Adam lies unconscious on the beach with the sounds of the jungle all around him. Oleandra, an exotic and sloe-eyed seductress, dances through the brush to the sound of jungle drums, accompanied by her gentlemen. They stop when they see Adam. She moves to him and cautiously touches him.)*
OLEANDRA. Are you alive?
ADAM. *(Stirring slightly.)* Gildoray. Isobel. My babies.
OLEANDRA. A madman. Throw him into the pit. Or toss him back into the drink. Let the tempest finish what it started. *(The gentlemen move to grab Adam. He rises weakly to his knees.)*
ADAM. Please, I pray you, I'm not mad — it's just the sea that's done this to me.
OLEANDRA. *(Her gaze softening.)* You're a well-spoken gentleman. And not foul of face. Tell me: what misfortune has cast you upon my shores? *(The memory of the shipwreck slowly washes over Adam's face.)*
ADAM. How I despise the weight of these words on my tongue. For to expel them into the air means this is not some sad nightmare but a true horror in the waking world. I am the world's great fool. I was chasing a kingdom that now I see is only a shadow. And in pursuit of this phantom I drowned my wife and my children. I

was robbed of one family at birth. I used to believe this was the worst of all crimes. But now I see I was sorely mistaken. For I've murdered the family I only just won.

OLEANDRA. Unlucky man.

ADAM. I should wrap these vines around my neck. I should hang myself from this tree. *(Tenderly Oleandra goes to Adam and embraces him.)*

OLEANDRA. You need do nothing so dire. You're safe now. You've landed in the jungles of Ygrippa. And I'm the empress of this country. You may rest here with us till the end of your days.

ADAM. Today is the end of my days. I deserve no more air.

OLEANDRA. Nonsense. Have you eyes to gaze upon me? Have you hands to caress my cheek? It's a mortal sin to stop your own heart from beating. Only Nature has that privilege. For her own private reasons she's chosen to preserve you. And she's delivered you to me. You must forget all the troubles that have befallen you.

ADAM. How is that possible? *(Oleandra smiles. She reaches up and picks a plum off a tree.)*

OLEANDRA. Oh, my child, it's so simple. Here. Take a bite of this plum.

ADAM. What will happen if I do?

OLEANDRA. As the juice travels down your throat, it will cleanse your body and mind of all its history. You'll recall no moment before this.

ADAM. This is some dark sorcery.

OLEANDRA. It's no sorcery. It's just Nature. She wants your arms to work her soil. She wants your breath to make her acacias bloom. And she wants you to lie with all the women you meet, so they might be delivered of babies who can be her new servants. Nature cares nothing for your heartbreak. So why should you?

ADAM. But I'm a murderer. How can I endeavor to wipe that away?

OLEANDRA. The day I washed up in this jungle I ate one of these plums. And then all the random sorrows and sins that deposited me here — I simply forgot them. All I hear is the crash of the waves against the shore and all I smell is the perfume of the jonquils and all I see is your hair tumbling across your brow. I devour at least ten of these plums every day. Now I even forget

things while they're happening. *(She holds out the plum to him. He considers, then takes it from her, staring at it in astonishment.)*
ADAM. If I take one bite, I'll forget about Gildoray forever?
OLEANDRA. And your wife and your children are already drowned. It will do no good to drown them doubly with your tears.
ADAM. What you're offering me — perhaps it's the greatest mercy.
OLEANDRA. I'll make you a new kingdom. You'll be untroubled for all your days. Grant me one kiss to bind us. *(Oleandra leans in and kisses Adam passionately on the mouth. Adam responds. All of a sudden he pulls away and stares at her in horror.)*
ADAM. But how deathly your mouth feels upon mine. You're nothing more than a corpse walking the earth.
OLEANDRA. *(Her face slowly hardening.)* Stay your tongue a little lest you mar your fortunes.
ADAM. Now I see: no matter how much pain I feel, there's a far worse pain that comes from feeling no pain at all. *(Oleandra signals to her gentlemen. They take hold of Adam.)*
OLEANDRA. If you deny me, I'll cast you into this pit. I'll make you my prisoner until the rats tear the last flake of skin off your bones. Is that truly what you prefer? *(Adam takes the plum in his fist and squeezes it till the juice runs through his fingers and drips in a puddle on the ground.)*
ADAM. To sit alone in the dark until the end of my days, weeping for my lost family? This is the only destiny I deserve. I welcome it.
OLEANDRA. Very well, then — you've condemned yourself. *(The gentlemen hurl Adam into the pit and bolt the gate over him. Adam huddles in the shadows.)*
ADAM. Oh, my children, I'll remain here in this prison forever, and you'll be my only companions. I'll conjure you up as you would've been. Today you stand to take a fumbling step. Tomorrow your first words will form themselves on your lips. Your ghosts will flourish and grow and every day you'll torment me for stopping your hearts. And when there is mercy and my end finally comes, you'll close my eyes and sprinkle dust upon my chest, for children are meant to bury their fathers. *(Adam's voice goes silent. For a moment all is black and quiet. Suddenly the gate is kicked open. Bartholomew, a haunted young prince, stands in the sunlight. Next to him stands a beautiful princess named Euralie. Her eyes are closed and*

she is fast asleep. Adam stares up at Bartholomew.)
BARTHOLOMEW. A survivor.
ADAM. Am I still alive?
BARTHOLOMEW. You must be a true hero to have sustained yourself in this pit.
ADAM. I ate the carcasses of rats and I drank the juice of beetles. I'm no kind of hero. I'm just a craven survivor.
BARTHOLOMEW. And more fortunate than you know. A plague wiped out this entire country. You can't tell one skeleton from another up there. *(Adam climbs out of the pit to reveal that his face is wrinkled and his hair is white. Bartholomew considers him in amazement.)*
ADAM. Then I'm the only one left?
BARTHOLOMEW. Twice the hero I thought you were, for such an old man to survive all this. *(Adam puts his hands to his face.)*
ADAM. So I've turned ancient?
BARTHOLOMEW. Poor man — I fear you've been living too long beneath the earth.
ADAM. This doesn't make any sense. Why have I been condemned to live?
BARTHOLOMEW. Too well I know your grief. For I've come here to die myself.
ADAM. What sorrows are harrowing you? And who is this princess?
BARTHOLOMEW. I was betrothed to her. But a jealous old sorcerer also desired her. He cast a spell over her — now her eyes cannot see, her ears cannot hear, and her voice is silenced.
ADAM. Someone must entreat the sorcerer to lift the curse.
BARTHOLOMEW. In my fury I ran him through with my sword. And alas the spell perished unbroken with him.
ADAM. Is there truly no way to rescue her?
BARTHOLOMEW. I've been told that in the desert plains there grows a lily whose nectar has the power of resurrection. But I've been searching for that flower so many years now — I no longer believe that it even exists. I'll surrender my quest here.
ADAM. *(Considers him very closely.)* There's no need for you to despair. I'll travel with you and your princess till we find this flower.
BARTHOLOMEW. But why? I'm nothing to you.

ADAM. You've unearthed me. And if I am to walk in the world again, I must be of some use in it. *(They scale a mountain. The sun shifts direction in the sky.)*

BARTHOLOMEW. I fear for my kingdom, abandoned without me.

ADAM. What is your kingdom? An imaginary line drawn around an oblivious piece of terrain. All to contain a mass of incompatible souls. You're on the noblest mission now. You're preserving your love. *(Day turns into night as they reach the top of the mountain.)*

BARTHOLOMEW. The tones of her voice and the caress of her fingertips — they're vanishing from my recollection. And as soon as I forget what I loved about my princess, I'll forget even that I loved her.

ADAM. She's your wife. If you abandon her, you abandon yourself a thousand times over. *(The sun pours down as they stagger, exhausted, down the mountain.)*

BARTHOLOMEW. She's not my wife anymore. She's a monster to me. Why won't you let me abandon her? Why won't you just let me die?

ADAM. Never again will I surrender even one of my traveling companions.

BARTHOLOMEW. But this journey will never end.

ADAM. Open your eyes. *(Adam and Bartholomew stand in the middle of the desert. Bartholomew stares about him in amazement.)*

BARTHOLOMEW. We have arrived.

ADAM. Is this the flower you were seeking?

BARTHOLOMEW. This is it exactly.

ADAM. Let's restore your wife. *(Gently Adam lays Euralie on the ground. Bartholomew picks the flower and squeezes its juice onto Euralie's eyes. For an agonizing moment nothing happens. Then she reaches out to Bartholomew.)*

EURALIE. Are my eyes opened again? Are my hands free to embrace you?

BARTHOLOMEW. It's true, my princess, you're reborn. *(With some effort Euralie rises to her knees. Bartholomew embraces her. Adam looks on.)*

EURALIE. Oh, my love, what trials you must have suffered to redeem me.

BARTHOLOMEW. *(Extends his arm to Adam.)* Here's your true savior. Many times on our journey I lost faith. He always kept hold of you.
EURALIE. *(Stares at Adam in wonder.)* You're a stranger. Why have you sacrificed so much to rescue me?
ADAM. You were in my path.
EURALIE. I'm quite sure there's more to the story than that.
ADAM. You needn't be burdened with my history. The world is made up of nothing but sorrows and losings and fools like me.
EURALIE. Sorrows and losings and fools there are plenty. But there are wonders here, too, and resurrections. You must not despair of this place. *(Kisses him lightly on the forehead.)* There. I've cast a spell over you. Now all your wounds will be healed. Just as you've healed mine.
BARTHOLOMEW. Please come home with us to Magritta so we might pay you more worthy tribute.
ADAM. I'm grateful to you. But I don't belong to any country. I'm afraid this is where we must part.
EURALIE. You'll be remembered always in my prayers. *(They head out of the desert. Adam stares after them, utterly spent. We become aware that the prairie around him is full of hermits sitting beneath bushes and crouched behind rocks. Hanif, a chatty hermit, hobbles past the shrub against which Adam is resting.)*
HANIF. I say: are you planning to eat those berries?
ADAM. Kind sir — what country is this?
HANIF. This is no country. We're all hermits here. If you're not going to eat those berries, I wonder if I might have some. *(Hanif picks berries from the shrub and devours them ravenously.)*
ADAM. Please tell me: what brought you to this strange place? *(Behind them two hermits have gotten into a dispute over some food.)*
FIRST HERMIT. I want my coconut! Give me back my coconut!
HANIF. Well. I was a shoemaker in Myzil. Late one night I was hunched over my awl, fashioning a boot for our town preacher. And all at once I was repulsed by the feel of the leather between my fingers and the stench of the tar in my nostrils. And suddenly the very *idea* of shoes seemed utterly absurd to me. So I walked out of my house and I kept on walking and I haven't stopped since.
ADAM. And this is how you live now — with no monarch reign-

ing over you — with no boundary constraining you? *(Just beside them one hermit is beating another with a stick.)*
SECOND HERMIT. Mine! Mine! Mine!
HANIF. In truth this life is savage and horrible. We'd all murder each other for a grain of rice.
ADAM. Then why haven't you abandoned this place yourself?
HANIF. When I left home I deserted my bride and my sons. Surely my wife has never forgiven me and my sons have been taught to despise me. Why should I burden them any further by returning to them? So I entreat you, you must quit this desert, if there is any country willing to claim you.
ADAM. I used to believe that I was claimed by a country called Gildoray. All my life I was desperate for someone to direct me there.
HANIF. I've never laid eyes on that country. But the mad queen of Gildoray lives in that cave. *(Hanif gestures to the cave nearby. Adam stares at him in amazement.)*
ADAM. In this cave?
HANIF. I wouldn't go in there if I were you. *(But Adam is already wandering deep inside the dank and dim cave.)*
ADAM. Hello? *(An old crone flies at him from the blackness. She is dirty and feral and unfathomably ugly. She scratches furiously at Adam's eyes.)*
OLD CRONE. Get away from me! Don't touch me! I'll scratch your eyes out!
ADAM. *(Taken aback a moment.)* It's all right: you don't have to be afraid.
OLD CRONE. This is my food! Get your own food! Fuck you — trying to steal from an old lady!
ADAM. I don't want your food. I just want to speak with you for a minute. Will that be all right?
OLD CRONE. You want to have a pleasant *conversation?* Like *civilized* people? Well, find yourself a *chair,* I'll pour you some *tea* — fuck off! Get out of here! Fuck off!
ADAM. I have no wish to trouble you. I just want to ask you one question. Can you possibly be the queen of Gildoray?
OLD CRONE. The queen? I'm not queen of anything, except maybe this pile of *turds* I've got here. Bow down to me, my subjects. Look at me. I'm the queen of all this *shit.* Those hermits out

on the plain, sometimes they call me the mad queen. It's just a joke they play.
ADAM. *(Nods in understanding.)* Of course it could only be a joke.
OLD CRONE. Anyway what the fuck does it matter to you?
ADAM. It's of no matter at all, really. It's just, when I was a boy, I believed myself to be the lost prince of Gildoray.
OLD CRONE. Not another one.
ADAM. Another one?
OLD CRONE. Do you know how many thousands of boys make the pilgrimage to this desert? They all drop to their knees and call me mother. It seems like every man in the world believes that he's a lost prince. Pathetic if you ask me.
ADAM. I suppose it is. Do you see this ring? All my life I imagined that it was the royal signet of Gildoray. Isn't that the height of arrogance? Isn't that the depth of folly? *(The old crone takes Adam's hand and considers the ring. Her entire body freezes.)*
OLD CRONE. Please get out of here. Just go away.
ADAM. *(Stares at her very closely.)* I've traveled the four corners of the globe to rescue my mother from the wilderness.
OLD CRONE. *(Struggles for a long moment.)* If by some misfortune I *am* the queen of Gildoray — the last thing I'd want is for my son to make himself known to me. For the sight of him would snap me in two. So if I do recognize you as mine, by this jewel, or by other … affinities … I will never tell you.
ADAM. *(A moment, then, nods.)* I suppose I understand. *(Impulsively the old crone picks up a stone and a sharp stick from the ground. With the stick she quickly scratches some marks on the stone.)*
OLD CRONE. But if you are the lost prince of Gildoray — then your people are waiting desperately for you to reclaim your rightful place on the throne. And if such a place as Gildoray exists — it lies in this direction, across the sea, just beyond that horizon line. *(She hands the stone to Adam. Adam considers it. He nods. He steps to the cliffs at the edge of the sea. He turns back to her.)*
ADAM. If I am this lost prince — I will redeem my countrymen and my kingdom. And I will accomplish this in the name of my mother the queen, who sacrificed her own life so I might be delivered.
OLD CRONE. *(A moment, then, hisses and spits.)* Then get out of

here! Before I scratch your eyes out! Before I tear you limb from limb! *(Adam nods and dives into the water. The geographer appears holding the stone. He shows us the scratched markings on the flat side.)*
THE GEOGRAPHER. This stone was recently exhumed from an archeological dig. Upon close examination these markings reveal themselves to be a primitively drawn yet entirely accurate map depicting the cliffs of Kreitag and the surrounding Cerulean Sea. *(He steps over to the map depicting the island divided into one large country labeled* Amaranthia *and one smaller country labeled* Leocadia.*)* Now: it's absolutely essential that we consider the concurrent events taking place in the faraway nations of Amaranthia and Leocadia. One location of particular relevance to our purpose is this road, located here — *(Points to a spot on the map.)* — in the rocky plains of the northeast corner of Amaranthia. *(A blocky old coachman named Root spurs his horse down a pebbly road. All of a sudden Nicholeaus, a plucky, unwashed young ruffian, runs up in front of the carriage.)*
ROOT. Out of the way.
NICHOLEAUS. *(Holds out his hands in supplication.)* Pray, kind sir, have you any coins to spare for a beggar?
ROOT. I have coins, but none for you. Now move on before I spur my horse to run you down. *(In a flash Nicholeaus jumps on the coachman's rail. He unsheathes his knife and puts it to Root's neck.)*
NICHOLEAUS. I beg of you, sir, I don't wish to do this, but truly I'm starving. Please, just toss me a few coins, whatever you can spare, and I'll be merciful with you.
ROOT. *(Leans in conspiratorially.)* I'll tell you a secret: my passenger is Queen Amarantha, and she's traveling incognito with her Royal Guard through her kingdom. Should you try to rob her, her man will surely break your neck.
NICHOLEAUS. *(Helplessly.)* I'm nearly dead already anyway. What choice do I have? *(The door to the coach opens and Amarantha, icy and ruthless, emerges. At her side is her beefy and sadistic guard Johannes.)*
AMARANTHA. I grow weary of the same scenery out my window. Why are we stopped?
NICHOLEAUS. I'm sorry to trouble you, your Majesty, but I'm dying of hunger.

AMARANTHA. What concern is that of mine? *(She nods to Johannes, who strides over and grabs Root away from Nicholeaus. As Nicholeaus watches in shock, Johannes shoves Root violently to the ground.)*
JOHANNES. You fool. How could you let this child overpower you?
ROOT. *(Cowering in fear.)* I'm sorry, sir — he had his knife on me so fast, and I —
JOHANNES. You're not worthy to serve our queen. *(Johannes unsheathes his sword and runs Root through. Root dies. Nicholeaus watches open-mouthed.)*
NICHOLEAUS. I beg of you, your Majesty, please be merciful with me.
AMARANTHA. Tell me your name.
NICHOLEAUS. I call myself Nicholeaus when there's any call for introductions.
AMARANTHA. Well, Nicholeaus: if you're so hungry why don't you sell the chain around your neck? That would fetch you a few shillings at least.
NICHOLEAUS. *(Holds out the chain.)* This is one prize I'll not surrender. When I was a babe, and a fisherwoman plucked me from the jaws of the deep, this chain was clutched tight between my fingers. Clearly it's a warrior's signet. I'm the son of a great tribe, cast at birth unwanted into the sea. But I'll prove myself worthy in my strength, so when they meet me again they'll be proud to claim me for their band.
JOHANNES. *(Strides toward Nicholeaus.)* Shall I dispose of him now, your Majesty?
AMARANTHA. *(Raises her hand.)* Stay your hand a moment. The boy is entertaining me. *(To Nicholeaus.)* But you've led such a hardscrabble life. How have you managed to keep this jewel from being stolen?
NICHOLEAUS. Through sheer vigilance, I suppose. Often when I was a boy the fishermen tried to lift it off me. I'd bite their fingers till I drew blood.
AMARANTHA. You're quite a warrior then. I'd like to see this talent in action. Johannes: you're free to do what you want with him. *(Immediately Johannes attacks Nicholeaus, wrestling him to the ground.*

Nicholeaus is nearly pinned but manages to wriggle through Johannes' legs. Johannes comes at Nicholeaus again, but Nicholeaus slips behind him and gives him a hard chop at the base of the neck. Johannes goes down in pain and Nicholeaus stands above him, twisting his arms.)
JOHANNES. *(Cries out in pain.)* I'm bettered.
AMARANTHA. That's readily apparent. And I must say, it's very disappointing. But Nicholeaus: you're far more masterful than I imagined.
NICHOLEAUS. Please — your Majesty — if you'll but give me a few coins from your purse, I'll show him mercy.
AMARANTHA. *(Muses a moment.)* I have a better proposition for you. If you kill him, I'll give you *all* my purse.
JOHANNES. *(Stares at Amarantha in shock.)* My Queen?
AMARANTHA. You see, I'm about to declare war on my son Leocad. For his eighteenth birthday I made him a present of nearly half my kingdom. And he's proven himself entirely unworthy of the gift. He's let the farmlands go fallow, he's let the basins drain dry, and he's spent the tributes of his loyal subjects on opium and whores. And when I demanded his abdication he had the gall to raise an army against me. I require a valiant soldier by my side to strategize the battles that are soon to rage.
NICHOLEAUS. Please don't make me kill him, your Majesty.
AMARANTHA. But you have no choice. For given the chance, Johannes will not be nearly so merciful with you. *(Indeed Johannes has maneuvered himself out of Nicholeaus' grasp. With a roar he knocks Nicholeaus to the ground. Johannes grabs his sword and attacks Nicholeaus. Nicholeaus slips out of his grasp, grabbing hold of Johannes' sword, running him through. Johannes falls to the ground, dead.)*
NICHOLEAUS. *(Stares aghast.)* I didn't want him murdered.
AMARANTHA. But you did it anyway. That's the sign of a true warrior. I'm proud to welcome you into my employ. But at the moment there's a more pressing matter to consider. It appears I'm in dire need of a coachman to carry me to my palace.
NICHOLEAUS. I'd be honored to convey you.
AMARANTHA. Excellent. And tonight I'll give a banquet in your honor, and we'll discuss the terms of your employment. *(The Geographer pulls down a map depicting the Isle of Briquez.)*
THE GEOGRAPHER. Here we have a map depicting the Isle of

Briquez. The legend here reads: "Come to the Isle of Briquez. Play our games of chance. Smoke our fine locally grown opiates. And indulge yourself with the most spectacularly talented courtesans in the civilized world." I assure you that this episode is of the utmost importance to our narrative and has not been inserted merely for the purpose of prurient titillation. *(Behind a billowing curtain the silhouettes of a man and woman making love can be seen. The lovers subside into stillness and the curtain is parted to reveal Leocad, a wastrel and scoundrel, staring up in awe at Marguerite, a lively, ingratiating courtesan.)*
LEOCAD. So beautiful.
MARGUERITE. *(With an ingenuous charm.)* You're sweet. I'll take the rest of my fee now. *(Marguerite climbs off the bed.)*
LEOCAD. Let me just look at you.
MARGUERITE. Is this your purse, over here, by your trousers?
LEOCAD. Take whatever you want. *(Marguerite brings the purse over to Leocad and sits down on the bed.)*
MARGUERITE. I'm only permitted to take what's due me. They're very strict about that here. No tipping. *(Leocad dumps the entire contents of his purse on to the bedside table.)*
LEOCAD. Will this be enough to make you mine for the rest of the night?
MARGUERITE. That should just about do it. Do you want some wine? Or how about a smoke? Help you forget your troubles.
LEOCAD. How do you know I have troubles?
MARGUERITE. Who doesn't have troubles?
LEOCAD. I don't think *you* have a single trouble in the world.
MARGUERITE. That's right — I don't. So tell me yours.
LEOCAD. *(Petulantly.)* It's all my mother's fault.
MARGUERITE. Poor baby.
LEOCAD. She's the Queen of Amaranthia. And on my eighteenth birthday she made me a present of almost half her kingdom. And just because I let a few fields go fallow and a bunch of peasants starved to death, now she wants to take back my land. I've raised an army — I'll go to war with her if I have to. Maybe I'll even take *her* kingdom for myself!
MARGUERITE. There, there. Don't overexcite yourself now.
LEOCAD. I've forgotten your name.

MARGUERITE. Marguerite.
LEOCAD. *(Stares at her, puzzled.)* Yesterday you told me your name was something different.
MARGUERITE. *(Smiles dreamily.)* Yesterday my name *was* something different. But you're Prince Leocad. That's the only name I care about tonight.
LEOCAD. Every man who's been to this island tells me about the astounding whores. Their names are Calliope or Bernadette or Therese. But they all have raven-black hair and hazel-blue eyes and a jeweled chain about their necks. I've just realized: they're all you.
MARGUERITE. Don't be silly. I'm no one at all.
LEOCAD. How is that possible?
MARGUERITE. *(Holds out the chain about her neck.)* This chain you admire — it's my prize possession. When I was a baby, I washed up on these shores with it clutched between my fingers. Clearly I'm a lost princess, cast upon the sea by a shipwreck. And in my home kingdom they've buried me and mourned me a hundred times over. And I won't be reunited with my family until we're all safe in the next life. So until then I'm no one at all and nothing will ever happen to me.
LEOCAD. *(Stares enraptured at her.)* Tell me, what would it cost to buy you away from here forever?
MARGUERITE. You don't have that kind of money in your purse.
LEOCAD. *(With a wave of his hand.)* I can acquire it easily enough: I'll just raise taxes again. And nothing would give me more pleasure than to tell my mother I've squandered all my tributes on a whore. So what do you say? Will you have me?
MARGUERITE. *(Very brightly.)* I suppose it would be something to do. *(The Geographer appears holding the stone in his hand.)*
THE GEOGRAPHER. Now let's return to Adam's journey, as I'm afraid we've literally left him hanging in midair. Ciphering the indentations on this stone, we can surmise that he leapt off the cliffs of Kreitag and began swimming due east until he found himself in what was then an uncharted region of the Cerulean Sea. *(As Adam swims the sea, he comes upon a watchtower sticking up out of the waves. Mamillius, an endearingly stiff young soldier, stands guard atop the tower.)*

MAMILLIUS. Did you lose your ship?

ADAM. I never had one to start with.

MAMILLIUS. You might want to take a breather before you try and swim the rest of the sea. *(Mamillius extends his arm to Adam and helps him up into the tower.)*

ADAM. It's a ridiculous thing to do, I know, but I was trying to get home and I ran out of land.

MAMILLIUS. *(Gives Adam a small salute.)* I'm happy to be of service. I'm Private First Class Mamillius in His Majesty's Royal Guard.

ADAM. I'm very grateful to you. But where's your country? And why does the Royal Guard need a watchtower in the middle of the sea?

MAMILLIUS. *(After a moment's hesitation.)* Well. I'm sorry to say this didn't use to be the sea. There was a great storm. And a massive wave came up out of the west. I saw it bearing down on us, but there was nothing I could do — it was beyond the power of any army to fight. I watched as it consumed all the villages and forests and fields below me. And now this tower and I are all that remains of Gildoray.

ADAM. Gildoray?

MAMILLIUS. Did you know my country?

ADAM. I believe I was born here. But I have no memory of the place. I've been told it was a land of unsurpassed beauty.

MAMILLIUS. *(Nods eagerly.)* It was a beauteous country, fair and verdant, bordered on the east by an untameable wilderness and on the west by an emerald sea. From the highest peak of the Veritian Mountains you could see as far as the Maltavi Plains. And if you waded downstream in the Falani River, you could reach up and pick an apple from the orchard on the edge of the Ingreven Forest.

ADAM. It sounds like a paradise.

MAMILLIUS. It would've been but for our king. He made all of us his prisoners and his slaves.

ADAM. A hero should've come to rescue you from this tyrant.

MAMILLIUS. My mother used to tell me the story of our lost prince. How one day he would return to break our chains and reclaim his throne. Now I understand that he was only a tale to tell children before they fell asleep so they wouldn't despair of the day to come.

ADAM. I must confess to you, I believe I may be your prince. *(He holds out his hand to Mamillius. Mamillius stares at the ring on Adam's finger. He falls to his knees and kisses Adam's feet.)*
MAMILLIUS. Your Majesty.
ADAM. *(Raises him to his feet.)* You mustn't fall on your knees for me. I was too long on my voyage here. I failed to save my people.
MAMILLIUS. But I'm blessed a hundred times over, that I'm permitted to gaze upon my true king before I perish.
ADAM. There's no need for you to perish here. Come away with me.
MAMILLIUS. I can't swim.
ADAM. I'll carry you.
MAMILLIUS. There's no land for miles. You can't possibly bear me for so vast a distance.
ADAM. I can swim for leagues, if that will deliver one of my countrymen.
MAMILLIUS. I'm not sure I want to be delivered. Gildoray is my home. I can't bear to abandon it. Maybe before I die, the flood waters will subside just enough that I might catch a glimpse of the tops of the trees I used to climb. I beg of you, stay here with me, your Majesty. This is your kingdom. You're home at last.
ADAM. Since I am your king, I command you: you mustn't make your kingdom your grave. *(Mamillius takes one last look at the sea below. Then he nods. They jump from the tower. On the beach, three scrubby fishermen tug at their net, pulling Adam and Mamillius in to shore.)*
FIRST FISHERMAN. I knew we'd catch some fish today: there was a red sky last night.
SECOND FISHERMAN. A red sky at night doesn't mean fish. It means a storm is coming.
THIRD FISHERMAN. No, no — a red sky at *morning* means a storm.
SECOND FISHERMAN. Are you sure?
THIRD FISHERMAN. Red sky at night, sailors delight. Red sky at morning, sailors take warning. *(The fishermen open their net to reveal Adam and Mamillius inside. They groan with disappointment.)*
ADAM. I'm afraid we've wrecked your net.
SECOND FISHERMAN. We haven't caught anything all morn-

ing. At least you provided us with some momentary excitement.
THIRD FISHERMAN. Here, I'll cut you free. *(He takes out his knife and cuts the net around Adam and Mamillius.)*
ADAM. Pray tell me, what land are we in now?
FIRST FISHERMAN. This is a fishermen's principality called Parnelia. There's a village just up that hill.
ADAM. *(Turns to Mamillius.)* Perhaps this is a decent place for you to start again. For I must leave you.
MAMILLIUS. You're not coming with me?
ADAM. I'd only be a burden to you. But you'll need money. *(Takes the ring from his finger.)* Sell this in the market: you'll fetch a good price for it.
MAMILLIUS. I can't take this.
ADAM. I have no country anymore. So this is my last command. *(Mamillius considers a moment. He accepts the ring from Adam.)*
MAMILLIUS. But where will you go from here? *(Adam considers a moment. He turns back to the fishermen.)*
ADAM. Tell me — where does this road lead?
THIRD FISHERMAN. North. To the tundra.
ADAM. Then this is the perfect path for me to take. I will make that country my home. For I am an orphan and a castaway again. I am as blank as a snowdrift. I wish you good fortune on your journey.
MAMILLIUS. *(Gives Adam another small salute.)* God speed you then, my lost prince. *(Adam turns and heads down the path. Snow starts to fall, harder and harder. The wind whips violently across his face. He pulls his clothes around him, shivering from the bitter cold. Gradually the wind dies down and the snow stops falling. Adam cups his hand to his forehead to peer off into the distance at a hunched, decrepit figure wandering toward him.)*
ADAM. I can't believe there's another wayfarer in this wasteland. *(The figure turns: it is Isobel. Her eyes are hollowed out, her hair has gone white, and her clothes are in tatters.)*
ISOBEL. I'm no wayfarer: this is my home.
ADAM. Isobel?
ISOBEL. *(Turns to look at Adam.)* Finally I've gone mad: I'm having visions of the dead.
ADAM. I fear that I too have taken leave of my senses. For it's not possible that you've preserved yourself in this wilderness.

ISOBEL. Oh, this place isn't so bad. Quickly the ice blisters your feet and the winds crack your face. And then you become something *of* this country. And you surrender altogether the notion that you were ever anything else. And that's so terribly pleasant.
ADAM. *(Stares at her in wonder.)* Then are the Heavens merciful? Are you still drawing breath?
ISOBEL. *(Very serenely.)* Hush now. You're merely a fancy of my fevered mind.
ADAM. I know at least that I'm no spirit. See, I'm solid to the touch. *(Adam reaches out and touches Isobel's hand. She stares at him.)*
ISOBEL. Oh, no, he's real.
ADAM. Oh, my love — have we reclaimed each other at last? *(Violently Isobel pulls away from him. Adam stares, uncomprehending.)*
ISOBEL. *(In pain and fury.)* How dare you come for me now! Haven't you tortured me enough? Can't you at least let me die in peace?
ADAM. I fear you've been too many years in this winter — !
ISOBEL. You ripped my babies from my arms! You cast me into the sea! You abandoned me to the wind and the rain!
ADAM. I lost you for too long, I know —
ISOBEL. I washed ashore on an island of cannibals. They fattened me up to devour me. I dug a tunnel underground to escape. I was bitten by a rat and got infected with the rabies. My heart slowed to a crawl and my body was dumped into a mass grave. I had to claw my way out through acres of rotted flesh.
ADAM. How much you've endured all these years!
ISOBEL. And somehow I landed in this country, and an old tramp told me I could reach Gildoray if I just traveled across the snow. But now I fear it was all a cruel hoax for I've been lost and wandering here forever and Gildoray is not to be found.
ADAM. If you've managed to survive in the face of all these torments, then surely you're a lioness.
ISOBEL. Yes, one thing I've learned from all this, I'm far stronger than I ever could've possibly imagined. But really I'd rather not have learned that. Truly I'd rather not have known. *(With a harsh laugh.)* So did you find Gildoray? Are you a king now?
ADAM. I *did* find Gildoray. But the place wasn't there anymore.
ISOBEL. So it might as well have been imaginary. And in all your

travels, you were never by chance reunited with our children?
ADAM. No.
ISOBEL. So we've both come to nothing. *(Isobel bobs and weaves a little on the snow. Adam goes to her and tries to hold her but she eludes his grasp.)*
ADAM. Not nothing, never nothing — for now we've reclaimed each other. Here, let me remove you from this place. If you're too weak I'll carry you. *(Adam takes hold of Isobel but she slips through his grasp and falls weakly to the ground. Adam kneels down next to her helplessly.)*
ISOBEL. You'll only be bearing a corpse in your arms. Don't you see? All that keeps me here are a few practicalities of breath and heartbeat, and they'll be surrendered soon enough.
ADAM. For the life of me I can't comprehend how this came to pass, for to the depths of my soul my only wish was to build a kingdom for you and our babies.
ISOBEL. But this was never even necessary. The day you washed up on my father's shores you built a kingdom for me in your mind's eye and I gladly would've lived there with you till the end of my days. Why wasn't that enough for you? Why wasn't I enough?
ADAM. You should've been everything. *(Gently she lifts her hand to caress his cheek.)*
ISOBEL. My poor castaway — when you carried me out of my father's palace it was the only blessed hour of my life. You have my endless gratitude for that. And I only wish — *(Isobel dies. The snow softly starts to fall again. A giant red-winged hawk descends from the sky and circles for a moment before he alights near Adam. When he speaks his voice is kind and gentle.)*
RED-WINGED HAWK. You'll freeze to death if you stay here. *(Adam clutches Isobel tightly.)*
ADAM. Get away from her! You scavenger! Can't you wait even a minute before you tear her to pieces?
RED-WINGED HAWK. *(With tremendous forbearance.)* I'm no scavenger. Climb on my back and I'll carry you away.
ADAM. *(Stares at him in wonder.)* How can we understand each other?
RED-WINGED HAWK. I try to talk with men all the time. But generally only the crazy ones understand me.

ADAM. And I suppose I must be mad by now. Will you carry my wife with you too? I want to give her a decent burial.
RED-WINGED HAWK. I'm only strong enough to bear one of you. And she's a shell. Please let me take you away from this place. *(Adam considers a moment. He kisses Isobel gently on the brow, removes her chain, places it about his own neck, and climbs on the back of the hawk. The hawk rises into the sky.)*
ADAM. What a marvelous thing it is to abandon the ground.
RED-WINGED HAWK. Yes, we often wonder how you manage it, consigned there all your lives. Hold on tight.
ADAM. *(Peers down at the ground.)* We've traveled so far so fast. Why didn't I hitch a ride on your back when I was a boy? I would've found Gildoray in no time.
RED-WINGED HAWK. Is that the place you were looking for? We always wondered. You know, you're the one we like to watch the most. We all talk about you. There's a rock dove who saw you wandering in the desert. There's a wood-finch who swears he caught sight of you in the jungle. You've been everywhere.
ADAM. Everywhere? Have I? Truly? *(Pause.)* You've been watching me all these years?
RED-WINGED HAWK. It's my favorite pastime. Without you the sky would get pretty monotonous. But I could never determine your purpose in wandering so ceaselessly. Finally I decided you were put on earth simply for my amusement.
ADAM. It's the only good reason I can think of.
RED-WINGED HAWK. Where are you bound now?
ADAM. There's nothing left in this world that binds me.
RED-WINGED HAWK. Then where would you like me to take you?
ADAM. What's that place down there?
RED-WINGED HAWK. It's a country I believe called Amaranthia. But you don't wish to land there. The place has been at war with itself for years now. The landscape is littered with corpses.
ADAM. Then I'll rest there among the dead. *(Adam lets go of the hawk and plummets to the ground. On a grass hill far below a battle is about to begin. Amarantha stands imperiously, flanked by Nicholeaus. Facing her is a brazenly smirking Leocad. Hanging on his shoulders like an ornament is Marguerite. Attending Leocad is a royal mapmaker.*

Adam falls from the sky and lands on the ground with an unceremonious thump. They stare at him. Adam opens his eyes and looks around.)
AMARANTHA. Generally I don't put too much stock in this sort of thing, but when old men start falling from the sky, surely the gods aren't smiling on us.
ADAM. At last: I'm home.
AMARANTHA. This is no one's home, old man. This is a battlefield.
LEOCAD. Indeed I am about to call my men to arms. You should make yourself scarce if you don't wish to be carrion yourself.
ADAM. I'm afraid this has to be my home. This is where I've landed. And I'm too tired to travel any farther.
NICHOLEAUS. This poor man has lost his sway over his senses.
MARGUERITE. Do you know your name, good sir?
ADAM. Adam is my only name. I thought I would claim another one day, but I was sorely mistaken.
AMARANTHA. A madman. Let him linger here if he wants. What's one more carcass in the middle of all this carnage?
LEOCAD. We've been slaughtering each other for too long now. I offer you one last chance to abdicate this folly. *(Leocad signals to the mapmaker, who unfurls the familiar map depicting the territory divided into one large country labeled* Amaranthia *and one smaller country labeled* Leocadia. *He indicates the map.)* Here is your country. And here is mine. And the boundary between them lies right at our feet. Let me rule over my territory as I see fit. Otherwise I'll charge up this hill and take away your entire kingdom.
AMARANTHA. If you *attempt* that, your army will be decimated and by nightfall your corpse will be swinging from the highest tree!
LEOCAD. If you truly wish your own death I will deliver it to you.
AMARANTHA. What a mockery of a man you are! I should've smothered you in your cradle! You'd even bring your whore to the bargaining table!
MARGUERITE. *(Outraged.)* I am not — I'm a lost princess cast on the sea by a shipwreck!
LEOCAD. *(Draws his sword on Amarantha.)* I'll pierce you though the heart right now and make an end of it!
NICHOLEAUS. *(Draws his sword on Leocad.)* Take one step across our border and you'll have to deal with me.
LEOCAD. I'd be happy to make sport of you, you mouse, you

pipsqueak — !
NICHOLEAUS. *(Rocked to the core.)* I'm a warrior and I'm the son of a warrior!
LEOCAD. *(Yells down the hill.)* Call my men to arms. Let the battle begin.
ADAM. Is there no rest for me at all? I only wish to stand still. Can I please stand still, just for a moment?
AMARANTHA. Will someone run this man through?
NICHOLEAUS. *(Draws his sword on Adam.)* I pray you, sir, I don't wish to murder you, but unless you quit this place at once I'll have no choice.
ADAM. *(Looks up at Nicholeaus.)* Are you my executioner? This is only just. Ages ago I scattered my son upon the sea. He would be of your years now. He would have your vengeance in his eye. Perhaps you are his wraith come to avenge his death.
NICHOLEAUS. *(Shoving Adam to the ground.)* I tender you mercy and you do nothing but mock me.
ADAM. I don't mean to mock you — I merely give myself up to you.
NICHOLEAUS. In the hour of my birth I was cast unwanted into the ocean. You make sport of my origins to hasten your own end.
ADAM. I offer my neck to your sword. And in exchange take this chain as my gift. My son would've worn one just like it had he lived. *(Adam unclasps the chain and holds it out to Nicholeaus. Nicholeaus stares at it. He freezes.)*
NICHOLEAUS. He wears it still. *(Adam looks up at him. Marguerite puts her hand to her mouth.)*
MARGUERITE. Pray tell me, sir: in that same cursed hour was your wife delivered of a baby girl?
ADAM. Indeed she was. Alas my daughter too was lost to the waves.
MARGUERITE. *(With a rush of emotion.)* If I were her ghost I would not seek vengeance. I would fall to my knees and embrace my father. I would entreat my brother to put away his sword. And you would know me by the chain about my neck. *(She falls to her knees. Adam stares at his children in wonder.)*
ADAM. Are you mine? *(Adam extends his arms to his children. They move toward him. Amarantha cries out in fury.)*
AMARANTHA. Not one step closer, Nicholeaus. It's death for

you to consort with my son's whore.

LEOCAD. *(Draws his sword on Nicholeaus.)* Cross my border and I'll happily remove you from your head.

MARGUERITE. *(Turns desperately to Leocad.)* My dear prince. You rescued me and took me as your own. I'll forever be your servant. But allow me one request — please relinquish my father and my brother to me.

NICHOLEAUS. *(Kneels before Amarantha.)* My Queen. You plucked me from the jaws of starvation. Always I'll owe you my life. But I beg of you — don't deny me my family.

LEOCAD. But I will not let that mercenary into my country.

AMARANTHA. And I will not permit that whore to set foot on my land.

LEOCAD. I cannot compromise this war for your celebration.

AMARANTHA. Indeed it would've been far wiser for you to make this reconciliation on less bloody ground.

ADAM. Tell me, where can we go? For I've traveled the world over, and there's no place safe in it. I've been swept away by hurricanes. I've battled pirates and warriors and monsters. And I was just trying to get home. Now I've reclaimed my children at long last. Can you not put down your swords even for a day? Will you not abandon this war just until the sun rises tomorrow? For if I cannot be granted but a few hours to rest with my family — then this life is cruel and barbarous beyond reason.

MAPMAKER. *(Raises his hands.)* My lieges. I believe there is a solution that will satisfy both monarchs without compromise or capitulation. For today only let these two nations be united into one new country. With your permission I'll draw up a map to authenticate this land. I'll christen it Adamus in honor of this old man. Thus he'll be granted one day to rest with his children by his side. And when dawn comes I'll draw up another map, dividing the territory asunder once again, and the war will commence as before. *(Amarantha and Leocad consider this for a tense, silent moment.)*

LEOCAD. This is acceptable to me. Draw up the map.

AMARANTHA. Very well, old man — until daybreak, this is your country. *(Amarantha, Leocad, and the mapmaker head down into the valley. Adam and Nicholeaus and Marguerite remain on the hill in the fading light of day. They consider each other for a long silent moment.)*

ADAM. I don't know how to begin.
NICHOLEAUS. *(Stares darkly at him.)* You could tell us why we were abandoned.
ADAM. I steered my ship into a storm. And that hurricane was midwife to your birth. She tore you from your mother's arms. I was sure the sea had claimed you. But you were both so desperate to live.
MARGUERITE. And did you drown our mother too?
ADAM. I condemned her to wander helpless in the wilderness. And I robbed you of her forever. I can never be pardoned for that.
NICHOLEAUS. But why did you have to desert us?
ADAM. My glass was trained on mirages. So I didn't even look upon your faces when you were born. If I had — surely I would've guided my vessel away from the tempest. You would've been mine all these years. Please tell me what's become of you. I know you're a soldier. And you're the wife of a prince.
NICHOLEAUS. I'm just a thief and a murderer. It's not such a noble calling. But it was the only way I could keep from starving to death.
MARGUERITE. And I'm nothing better than a whore. It was all I could do to survive.
NICHOLEAUS. When I was a boy I imagined I was the son of a great warrior. I don't suppose you're anything like that.
ADAM. A warrior? Perhaps I was, in my way. I bested an army of men to claim your mother. I cut off the head of a gryphon to redeem a child from the grave. Maybe I've bequeathed your fierceness to you. If I have, I'm grateful. It's a useful gift.
MARGUERITE. I'd whisper myself to sleep every night dreaming that I was a lost princess. But you're not any kind of king, are you?
ADAM. If I was ever bound for royalty, it's in a country that's not of this earth. But your mother was a princess pure-born. And I see her majesty everywhere in you.
NICHOLEAUS. It seems like the world has used you so cruelly.
ADAM. I put my oars in the water so I might one day claim my kingdom and abide in peace with my children at my side. And I've failed in this endeavor so spectacularly.
MARGUERITE. But you have a kingdom of your own tonight, Father. And you have your children at your side.

ADAM. I do, don't I?

NICHOLEAUS. *(Hot with righteous rage.)* But it seems such a cruel injustice that after your dreadful and ceaseless wanderings, you should be granted your family and your country for only one day.

ADAM. *(With a new comprehension.)* Oh, my children, this is such good fortune. In this world, it is the greatest good fortune.

MARGUERITE. *(Stares anguished at the sky.)* But what will become of us all tomorrow? For the day is waning so fast already.

ADAM. You mustn't curse the earth for turning. She only wishes to rock herself to sleep. For the earth is a wanderer herself, forever nodding away from the sun and back again. And she must be so weary of her travels, she must be so sick for comfort. She must long for the day when some gentle soul will hold her in his arms, so she can rest at last. *(Blanketed by his sad, bewildered children, Adam whispers consolingly to the earth beneath his feet.)* It's all right … I'm here … *(The stars begin to make themselves apparent in the firmament. The Geographer appears in front of the map depicting the country of Adamus.)*

THE GEOGRAPHER. And in the morning they drew up a map that once again divided the territory into the two warring nations of Amaranthia and Leocadia, and then they went up the hill and found the boy and the girl asleep in the arms of their father. And when they tried to rouse the old man they discovered that some time in the night his weary heart had stopped. At the entreaties of his children, a tomb was dug and the old man was buried beneath the very patch of earth which had sustained him for his final hours. A homily was said over his grave and then the war began again. And the country that for one day was known as Adamus simply ceased to exist. *(The moon rises, intensifying the focus of its light on Adam.)* Luckily this map somehow survived the floods and fires and tempests of the past several centuries. It stands as a testament to the wanderings of the lost prince of Gildoray even today, when the marks of his footsteps have vanished utterly in the sand. *(Adam places his hands on the face of the earth and whispers tenderly.)*

ADAM. I'm here … I'm here …

End of Play

PROPERTY LIST

Net, winch
Two large maps of Amaranthia and Leocadia
 (THE GEOGRAPHER, MAPMAKER)
Large map of Adamus (THE GEOGRAPHER)
Old book with maps (THE GEOGRAPHER)
Guitar (LORENZACCHIO)
Torch (ADAM)
Swords (XAVIER, XAVIER and VINCITORE, DARKLY JACK,
 SATURNIUS, ADAM, JOHANNES, LEOCAD,
 NICHOLEAUS)
Rope (XAVIER)
Log book (VINCITORE, THE GEOGRAPHER)
Ring (FERDINAND, ANSELM, ULRIKE)
Bucket of water (ULRIKE)
Bow and arrows (WILHELM, FERDINAND)
Wine cask (WILHELM)
Baby (OTTO, ADAM)
Rope (PIRATES, GUARDS)
Lanterns (ISOBEL and CINDRA)
Canteen (ISOBEL)
Ax (EXECUTIONER)
Whistle (SATURNIUS)
Two silver chalices, knife (HIGH PRIEST)
Map of Peregrine (THE GEOGRAPHER)
Knife (TOBIAS, NICHOLEAUS)
Charts and maps (THIRD SAILOR)
Two babies (NURSE)
Map of Octavian Ocean (THE GEOGRAPHER)
Plum (OLEANDRA)
Flower (BARTHOLOMEW)
Berries (HANIF)
Stick (HERMIT)
Stone and stick (OLD CRONE, THE GEOGRAPHER)
Map of Isle of Briquez (THE GEOGRAPHER)
Purse of money (LEOCAD)
Net (FISHERMEN)

SOUND EFFECTS

Waves
Music
Storm, thunder, water, wind
Jungle drums
Wind, snow